GYPSIES

OF THE
WHITE MOUNTAINS

HISTORY OF A NOMADIC CULTURE

BRUCE D. HEALD, PHD

Charleston — London

THE
History
PRESS

Published by The History Press
Charleston, SC 29403
www.historypress.net

Copyright © 2012 by Bruce D. Heald
All rights reserved

Unless otherwise noted, all images are from the author's collection.

First published 2012

Manufactured in the United States

ISBN 978.1.60949.824.5

Library of Congress CIP data applied for.

GYPSIES
OF THE
WHITE MOUNTAINS

To my close friends Deborah Herrington and Vinny Boulanger.

CONTENTS

FOREWORD

Historian Bruce Heald dwells in this book on the fascinating history of a stereotyped minority, the Gypsies, presenting not only the poetry of their world wanderings but also the misconceptions that can be viewed by exaggerations, especially nowadays, when Gypsies are, based on their citizenship, citizens of the European Union (EU).

The Gypsy minority has had, throughout history, a rough path. Most of the time, their adherence to an asocial structure, as well as their unusual practices, led European countries to take drastic measures against them. French politician Philippe Meunier is publicly requesting that the EU treaties be revisited, so Gypsy beggars can be sent back to their countries of citizenship (even though their citizenship allows them to travel freely anywhere inside the European Union boundaries).

This is something that former French president Nicolas Sarkozy was favorable toward while in office. Such approaches are not singular in the history of Europe; Bruce Heald's book covers this aspect in the twentieth century ("In 1939 and 1940, they were deported to Poland and the Nazi death camps, where thousands of Gypsies were sterilized and finally murdered because they did not conform") and also before that.

The author researches the connection of the minority (viewed as "citizens of the world") with America. Scholars maintain that Gypsies arrived in America during the colonial period, after being deported from several European countries. Since they were practicing fortunetelling and palmistry, which was forbidden, and were disruptive because of their nonconformity to local social structure, they were not quite welcomed by the colonial settlers.

The author contributes to an American understanding of Gypsies when presenting their social structure, as well as many interesting traditions that still govern their lives, like their interpretation of marriage, which is a family affair where women's chastity is a key concept; their occupations and practices, such as fortunetelling; and their stories and contacts with New Hampshire and the White Mountains.

His principle of fighting against stereotypes, which is a principle of his philosophy of life, made him study their story. It is not surprising to me that among the first phrases he writes about Gypsies is the following: "Gypsies are intriguing people. We have seen them, but we do not know them."

The reader obtains in Dr. Heald's book the flavor of the history of Gypsy minority, very artistic pictures and an accurate understanding of the interesting life and culture of their minority. Dr. Heald is one of the most significant public voices in New England, and his research on Gypsies is something that will be extremely relevant in Americans' understanding of the minority.

Cerasel Cuteanu, PhD
Adjunct Professor, Petrosani University
Senior Editor of the weekly newspaper *Gorjnews*, Romania

ACKNOWLEDGEMENTS

Thank you to Jennifer Anderson, Appalachian Mountain Club, Fritzie Baer, Grace H. Bean, Francis Belcher, Keith Bryar, Joanne Cram, Cerasel Cuteanu, Jack Frost, Calin Giurgiu, Ian Hancock, Deborah Herrington, Patrick J. Kiger, Laconia Motorcycle Club, Jean-Pierre Liegeois, Florin Petru Manole, John Marks, R.J. McGinnis, Butch Spare, John Spargo, Charlie St. Clair, Harold Wheeler and the White Mountain National Forest.

Chapter 1

ORIGIN OF THE GYPSY

Immigration to the New World

Many myths and legends have been written about the early Gypsies; however, few legends show the variety of notions of these people and their origin. Gypsies are intriguing people. We have seen them, but we do not know them. Gypsies are apt to worry us, for we do not understand them, leading to negative stereotypes. There are a few common beliefs, such as that the Gypsies are a people of remote ancestry who have a similar history. During the colonial period in America, mythical tales of the Gypsies made their entrance on the stage of history, especially in the New England area. There is no group more widespread over the earth than the Gypsies. Go wherever you wish in Europe, and you will find Gypsies everywhere. Some have recorded under 1 million numbering in Europe, and of these there may be at least 275,000 Gypsies in Hungary, 200,000 in Romania, 38,000 in Serbia and 52,000 in Bulgaria. In Great Britain, Ireland and Scotland, the numbers are unclear, but in America, there are possibly over 500,000 Gypsies.

Originating from Northern India, the Gypsies have become world wanderers. Their nomadic culture has not been due to their wandering as much as to the external pressures put upon them by local societies. In time these early Gypsies divided themselves into two groups and traveled in opposite directions. The Ben Gypsies traveled through Syria, Egypt and later throughout northern Africa; the Phen Gypsies traveled through the northern route and dispersed to Europe via Armenia and Byzantine Greece.

Two Gypsy boys. *Courtesy of Jean-Pierre Liegeois.*

Prior to the discovery of Indian origins of the Gypsies in the 1700s, myths and legends explained the origins and wandering behavior of these mysterious strangers. The Gypsies created and participated in building these myths either from a desire to confuse the non-Gypsies or by way of ignorance of their own culture.

Through their travels, the Gypsies were able to communicate their strange customs and also able to manipulate various host populations into believing that they possessed special mythical powers and magical talents. After wandering these many countries for more than two hundred years, the cult of Gypsies did not blend into any one country or church. This, in turn, made them prime candidates for a New World expansion, and they looked to the countries of Western Europe for settlement. It was in England, Ireland, France, Portugal, Turkey and Spain that they cultivated their influence and culture, but soon thousands upon thousands of Gypsies were deported to the western hemisphere of America.

For hundreds of years, the Gypsies endured as landless travelers throughout the world. From the time of their arrival in Romania from India, Gypsies were considered the slaves of the landowners, only to be emancipated in 1851. While in Romania, some of the Gypsies took to speaking a version of Romani called *Bayesh*, which can be heard in some of the songs by Gypsy groups recorded in Hungary. Nowadays, about 40 percent of the Gypsies still speak Romani, and many can still be seen traveling in lines of carts along the roads of Romania. The majority lived in the towns and villages in Romania, Transylvania and Hungary. Some live in large ornate houses but others in small buildings or trailers on scraps of lands on the edge of villages.

During the 1700s, they were subjected to hostility and violence. Decrees, laws and mandates often allowed the killing of Gypsies. For instance, Frederick William I of Prussia ordered all Gypsies over eighteen years of age to be hanged. A practice of Gypsy hunting was quite common—a game very similar to fox hunting. Even as late as 1835, there was a Gypsy hunt in Jutland (Denmark) that brought in a bag of over 260 men, women and children. The Gypsies have often been seen as intruders, nomads without a home amidst a society rooted in its ways. They were known to arouse mistrust, fear and even rejection.

Though the Gypsies had undergone many centuries of persecution, it remained relatively random until the twentieth century, when the negative stereotypes became molded into a racial identity, and these people were systematically slaughtered.

Romani family. *Courtesy photo edited by Harold Wheeler, Lnd., 1936.*

Romani friends of the author in Romania. Author is third from the left.

During World War II, the Gypsies shared the same suffering as the Jews and other minority groups. The Nazis considered them to be members of an inferior race. Thus, in 1938 a law was passed to counter the Gypsy threat. In 1939 and 1940, they were deported to Poland and the Nazi death camps, where thousands of Gypsies were sterilized and finally murdered because they did not conform and were considered an oddity to society.

According to Marlene Sway's *Familiar Strangers: Gypsy Life in America*, it has been suggested that approximately eight to ten million Gypsies have survived as citizens of the world. The Gypsies appear to be scattered and diverse, with no territory and few written records of their own. These people tend to rely on invisibility.

It is difficult to give a single description that embraces these people and their points of view. Legends and folklores show the variety of nations of Gypsy origins. In studying these tales, we begin to get the idea that Gypsies are a people of remote ancestry who have a common history—or at least some groups do, for the legends sometimes diverge.

It was not uncommon to see foreign travelers, peddlers, tinkers, Bohemians and Gypsies pass through the campsites in the White Hills of

New Hampshire. However, the Gypsies have led an almost invisible existence in America. The Gypsies have preserved their traditional way of life through networks of families, strict religious beliefs, a community-controlled structure and judicial system and their willingness to be nomadic in their occupations. The way Gypsies are treated has little to do with laws and more to do with the state of mind that is shaped by myths and stereotypes.

After spending several semesters teaching at Babes-Bolyai University in Cluj, Romania, I have become fascinated with many of the Gypsy traits, the working and social habits of the Romanian Gypsies. I have lived and camped among their community, and much of their lifestyle will be related in this book.

Within the content of this book, I may refer to the name "Gypsy" as it may refer to the whole mosaic of Romany peoples and their culture and way of life.

This is an adventure and celebration of a unique culture that was related to me while I either lived in Romania or personally traveled among them in the hills of New Hampshire. The American Gypsies of the early twentieth century certainly deserve our attention.

GYPSY IMMIGRATION TO THE NEW WORLD

Scholars generally believe that the Romani Gypsies arrived first in the New World as deportees from various European countries. Scholars of American Gypsies claim that the Romanies were deported from England and France to America during the colonial period.

The earliest Gypsies living in colonial America encountered antipathy on the part of colonial settlers. Despite this antipathy, the Gypsies remained and thrived in the early American southern colonies. Although they practiced the art of fortunetelling and palmistry, they were forbidden to tell fortunes for compensation or to practice palmistry. It was unlawful for any company or strolling group of persons to receive compensation or reward for the practice of telling fortunes and any other type of magical act.

As was stated earlier, a great deal of information indicates that the Gypsies in the United States number over 500,000. These statistics are uncertain. The official figures may differ based on the criteria used—who is a Gypsy—but this can be vague. Many of these people will not declare themselves as Gypsies, though they will sometimes use the general term *Bohemian* to distance themselves from the stigma used against them from past centuries of persecution. It is interesting to note that in 1885 the United States was forcing Gypsies to return to Europe.

The Gypsies in New England were often moving about in their nomadic groups and seen as threatening and disruptive. In most communities in New Hampshire they were not to be trusted, as their behavior appeared awkward and Bohemian in nature and appearance. This nonconformity to local social structure was a curiosity and was not welcomed.

The largest population of Gypsies may be found in the larger cities in America, such as Boston, Chicago, Seattle, Portland and Atlanta. It is often thought that Gypsies are exclusively urban settlers, when in fact half of the American Gypsy population is found in rural areas.

Many Gypsies do not like being categorized with the stereotypical label of "Gypsy," but rather, they prefer to remain as strangers to the non-Gypsies. It would seem that the less we know about them, the less we can abuse or harass them.

As the Gypsies wandered throughout New Hampshire during the nineteenth and early twentieth centuries, the local communities forced the Gypsies to set up their own campsites, which were mainly hidden from the main roads, in their horse-drawn Gypsy vans. Later, the Gypsies would be found living in trailer parks so that they could move on at a moment's notice. It was not unusual to find them camping in the center of an abandoned field or even behind a rubbish dump. Of course, these campsites were devoid of water and sanitary conditions. The Gypsies were not welcome for they were viewed as a threat, mysterious and mistrusted, a curiosity to the townspeople.

Even though they were good seasonal workers, their employers were cautious about the Gypsy behavior. These people were accepted as long as they remained confined to a specific area. The thinking of the townspeople was that the only good Gypsy was the mythical one—the one who does not really exist.

Times have changed, but this was to be expected. The social, political and economic climate of the country has made our society more complex. Gypsies, however, are accustomed to this environment, for they have long been trapped by their strange mythology and preconceptions about their behavior by outsiders (artistic and unrestrained but devoted to their traditions, family and folklore). They continue to be stereotyped as drifters and travelers, assumed to be dirty, thieving and untrustworthy. The non-Gypsy will set the image of the Gypsies as they please, and the Gypsies themselves will let them see what they expect to see as their lifestyle and behavior. The Gypsy has historically been saddled with negative attitudes.

There does not appear to be a happy medium between the myth of the handsome nomadic Gypsy and the Bohemian whose culture was seen but rejected as bizarre. The Gypsies have become increasingly disoriented. Once their world was the globe, but it now appears, in the minds of the non-Gypsy, they are limited to living in the shantytowns or campsites where few may see or associate with them.

It appears that the Gypsy culture and living habits are being forced to change. Once they lived in groups and families enlarged by marriages, but now they exist in smaller family units, severed from the cultural roots that they cherished and lived by.

The new American Gypsy movement appears to be changing the strange ways and customs that they brought from the old country. This change now enables them to ensure that society's view of their historic culture will not be imposed on them by non-Gypsies. *Kai Zas ame, Romale?* Roma, where are we headed?

Chapter 2

SOCIAL STRUCTURE

The Family

The structure of the Gypsy family was extremely important for their survival. Because the families were the first line of defense against outside negative influences, children were taught to remain apart from the dominant society and local community at the same time they were taught how to survive in it. The family's prime objective was to provide nurturing and emotional support; they were taught to function as one body and primary economic unit.

Without their particular family and kinship structure, the Gypsies could not function as a minority. Family cooperation is in the form of loyalty, sharing financial and personal resources and willingness to work cooperatively for long hours so as to accomplish economic stability and self-sufficiency.

The stability of the household is referred to as *tsera*, which also means "tent." The Gypsies were tent-dwellers until the 1930s, when the American Depression forced them into more permanent housing and they were put on welfare.

The Gypsy family also enjoyed living in isolation among their close relatives in their *vitsa*, which was considered an extension of families who followed the authority of a chief. The role of the family is and was to work as a collective group. However, any man who called himself "chief" or tried to act as a leader without prior consensus would, by definition, no longer be worthy of leadership. If a man was to have any chance of earning that leadership position, he must always behave wisely in his actions and stands, especially in formal gatherings.

Kalderari Romani boy, 1911.
*Courtesy photo edited by Harold
Wheeler, Lnd., 1936.*

The leader of a family is known as the *gadze*, and the leader actually represented no more than his family group. The family developed a loose organizational structure for governing itself. Traditionally, when several families traveled together they represented a band, which may be headed by a chieftain elected by the families. The powers of a chieftain would vary from one band to another, but one would not make decisions before consulting with a council of elders. The chieftain also sought advice from the woman in the band who focused on the welfare of the group's women and children.

Through the late nineteenth century and early twentieth century, the Gypsies were held responsible for any disorderly behavior in their communities, as they did not adhere to local laws. They were stereotyped as vagabonds, vagrants and armed highwaymen. The idea of Gypsy life was based on a mixture of vague fear and superstition traced back to European concepts of well poisoning, the spreading of a plague, witchcraft healing hands and, in the farmland, the burning of crops. These Gypsies were labeled as sorcerers, jugglers, pickpockets, tinkers and Bohemians.

Kalderash Roma's Camp, 1892. *Courtesy photo edited by Harold Wheeler, Lnd., 1936.*

The chiefs had strong responsibilities in order to maintain and enforce order as dictated in Romani culture. There may have been some renegades in the band, but they would surely endanger the security of all Gypsies. Such behavior from these renegades might include stealing, drunkenness and general disruptiveness in the local community. To prevent this, these renegades suffered the worst humiliation. They would be deprived of any honorable family and social life and would be forced to leave the community. An individual became more powerful with old age, good reputation and the establishment of effective authority in the families.

Through the years, the Gypsies have survived due to their ingenuity, and they have managed to adapt to their environment throughout the world. Many Gypsies have not only survived in their existence, but they have also become successful. They rely on family labor, hard work ethos and cooperation. Despite their lack of education throughout history, they have a strong understanding of the land and the people they live with, and consequently they have developed the ability to manufacture many commercial products that come from nature itself. Gypsies aggressively embrace the future regardless of the conflicts and hostility that may be ahead of them. To quote an elderly Romani Gypsy who demonstrates their confidence concerning the future: "You could put me down anywhere in the world and I could earn a living…You could even put me in the desert."

Sociologists will eventually come to realize the values, work ethos, vitality, creativity and richness of the Gypsy people. During the past 1,200 years of survival in this hostile environment, the Gypsies have developed a blueprint for endurance.

ROMANIES

The Romanies do not view themselves as Gypsies. In their language of *Romani*, there is no word to identify themselves as a whole. Gypsies were inclined to a nomadic, unconventional way of life, to be tinkers who move from one place to another—traders of goods. According to Jean-Pierre Liegeois, they may be defined by the views and attitudes of others, and they may find it difficult to think of themselves in terms of the totality that they form.

These Gypsies arrived in America during the early twentieth century. They are very intelligent and are most civil in their address. They make a living by farming or telling fortunes by palmistry, and some of them are believed to possess no inconsiderable means.

Like most families, the Gypsies treasure their social life. Even though their work and labor are important, it is considered to be an appendage of their personality, a necessary evil in their economy. What is more important is their sense of community. It is the Gypsies' belief that life should not be taken so seriously that you forget your heritage and the Gypsy culture.

EDUCATION OF THE YOUTH

Where, what and when do the Gypsies educate their children? Gypsy parents certainly want their children to learn how to read, write and do arithmetic;

A Gypsy smithy among Gypsies in Pittsburgh, January 1909.

however, sending their youth to school is not the primary means of education. When they are not forced to attend public schools by the welfare workers, Gypsy children are free to spend their time exploring the world around them. Much of their time is spent with their parents and other Gypsy families and children, and they are permitted to spend their idle time as they like.

MUSIC AND DANCE

Romani Gypsy music was, and still is, very important to their nomadic lifestyle, for they have long acted as wandering entertainers and tradesmen. Wherever Romanies live, they have become known as musicians. As the Gypsies traveled to other countries, they introduced many influences in their music, beginning with their Indian roots and adding elements of Greek, Persian, Turkish, Romanian, Czech and Slavic, as well as Western European, including German, French and Spanish forms.

Among the many styles of Romani dance, perhaps the most well known is the flamenco, the typical dance from Andalusia in the south of Spain. Other

Romani sheet music "Vaduvita Grasa."

styles are Ghawazee (Egyptian Gypsies), Rom (Eastern European Gypsies) and Tsjengui (Turkish Gypsies). The Turkish Gypsies crossed Turkey through the northern Black Sea region (Kara Deniz) and moved on to Trakya, passing Istanbul. In Istanbul, the Sulekule district is still famous for its Gypsy dances.

Romani music is characteristically vocal and very soulful, while the instrumentation varies widely according to the region the music comes from. Their music is considered passionate and is used for special celebrations and social affairs.

Most Romani Gypsy music is based on their folklore. The local music was adopted and performed, both instrumentally and vocally, and it slowly transformed into Romani styles, which were usually more complex. The music was performed at weddings, funerals, restaurants, special parties, coffeehouses and all other types of social gatherings. An important feature of their music was the belly dancing. The rhythmic accompaniment for their dancing was instrumental improvisation using such popular instruments as the clarinet, violin, accordion, panflute and piano.

Gypsy music is representative of a celebration around the campfire, a wedding, a social event, a festival or a dance. It expresses joy, sadness, grief, anger and pleasure. This medium of expression may be for a group of friends or for one's own company.

Spiritual

Spiritually, the Romanies did not embrace any organized religion, but they have a deep-seated spiritual belief. The Gypsy people believe that it is crucial to maintain a spiritual balance and that good and bad actions determine one's future. For example, respect for one's elders is considered essential to maintaining the dignity of the family. Romanies also believe in the importance of spiritual energy, which they think is drained when one spends too much time in the non-Romani world.

Marriage

The Romani families have very strict attitudes toward non-Gypsies (outsiders), and it is not acceptable for Gypsies to marry or be friends, work or generally socialize with someone outside their own ethnic group. According to historian Patrick J. Kiger, "Their tradition dictates that they avoid mixing too much with outsiders. Marriage between Romani and the non-Romani is considered taboo, and families are often reluctant to have their children educated in any western-style schools." The only remedy is to keep oneself in an all-Romani milieu, which is another reason why the Romanies tend to keep to themselves.

Marriage in the Gypsy tradition is still considered to be a family affair—a relation between family groups. Many of these marriages were and still are arranged; the community unites two families by the union of their two members. It is to encourage marriage among relatives and close Gypsy friends in the community; thus, marriage is very common within the extended kinship community. Most couples marry during their mid-teens. However, before they marry, they are not allowed to socialize alone, as great value is placed on the woman's chastity. This remains in effect until marriage; this is considered the ideal arrangement, because this marriage contract will bond their kin relationship.

When the marriage is arranged and the wedding set, it is celebrated elaborately. Of course, this depends on the wealth of the families participating. These weddings are most likely to last three or more days, and the expense for the ceremony will be the responsibility of the groom's family.

In the common wedding ceremony in America, the bride becomes part of the groom's family (symbolically) via a special dance known as a Balkan *kolo*. After the ceremony, the couple travels together to the reception, where the elders bless them with bread and salt.

For Gypsies in America, marriage licenses are ignored unless the couple needs a license for welfare purposes. As far as the wedding and reception are concerned, invitations are not necessary, so many friends and relatives generally attend.

According to Anne Sutherland's *Gypsies: The Hidden Americans*, "It is the custom in the United States for the Gypsy bride to live with her husband's family until she becomes a mother herself." It is expected that she will be subservient to her husband's family and assist with the family chores.

Chapter 3

GYPSY WORK ETHICS AND OCCUPATION

The Gypsies work because they have to. Their labors are not considered an end but rather a means to an end—their independence and mobility. In the United States, most Gypsies are willing to accept any kind of work that most Americans are not willing to do. Regardless of the nature of the work or how humiliating the labor, it is still an honest living and, in the Gypsy's mind, productive and honorable.

It is interesting to note that the Gypsies do not see welfare as charity; it is instead a method of outsmarting the non-Gypsy. They look on this income as compensation while they are waiting for work.

Being nomadic people, the Gypsies move more freely to available jobs, and they are dependent on seasonal occupations. These families establish regular circuits throughout Northern New Hampshire, usually spending limited seasonal time in one area before moving on. It is necessary for every member of the family to provide an income from more than one job or business for survival. They are always in search of new markets for their skills and services, such as work on farms, in the fields and in the forests as lumbermen. They may be found working as chimney sweeps, tinsmiths, in an iron foundry or tarring roofs and driveways. You may see the ladies telling fortunes, reading palms or cards, dancing, singing and entertaining whatever audience they may assemble for profit. With this in mind, being multi-occupational would afford the Gypsies a sense of job security.

This nomadic movement also enables the Gypsies to work during the four seasons. During the summer, they also concentrate their efforts on

Kalderari men near a tent, 1930. *Courtesy Florin Petru Manole's archive.*

places of recreation such as tourist resorts, amusement parks and country fairs working as fortunetellers or entertainers selling souvenirs. On the farm the men work in the fields and as local crop pickers; in the North Country, they become lumbermen. However, the men will only work the fields or forest if they are allowed to work and live only with their own kind, remain separate from other non-Gypsies and get paid with cash on a piece rate. The Gypsies feel more independent and prefer to contract their labors individually.

The Gypsy legend of their work ethics and industrial fortitude is their inventiveness. If a Gypsy *kumpania* (a member of a group of traveling families) is industrious, thrifty and aggressive, he will be successful, but if the *kumpania* is lazy and does not build the potential of his territory, then he has no one to blame but himself. The system ensures a just opportunity, but it does not ensure success.

The Gypsies guarantee one another the right to earn a living without internal competition. When a problem arises, the Gypsies resolve their problems, sometimes with violence. However, they invented another method

Gypsy family, 1905. *Courtesy photo edited by Harold Wheeler, Lnd., 1936.*

of dealing with renegade members who have been excommunicated from the community, for these members may be a danger to the group as a whole. To do this, the Gypsies gather members of the community who are in positions of authority.

The Gypsies have no age discrimination in the family; every member of the group contributes their fair share for the support of the family. The youth in the family contribute through their limited capabilities, such as begging and hawking wares like flowers, trinkets and pencils to tourists.

Women perform music by singing and dancing or they practice fortunetelling, palm reading or astromancy (horoscopes), but most of all they tend to the welfare of the family.

The elderly contribute to the family income by collecting welfare benefits. An example of this may be what they considered the Old Age Security (Social Security). If they are disabled physically, they may be entitled to government aid.

We Americans may view the Gypsies' way of life as being romantic and carefree, a culture of wanderers who come and go as they please with no permanent roots in a community. Think again, as they are nomadic because they need to survive on seasonal labor as mentioned earlier. This sacrifice of traveling from one area to another is not necessarily a sign of "wanderlust"; it is, however, an economic necessity that enables them simply to exist. They live from the land and have developed the ability to commercialize themselves via their talents and labor.

As much as we may look upon them as vagabonds, wanderers or Bohemians, they are successful because they depend on the family as a special unit of labor, cooperation and hardworking ethics. This gives them the competitive advantage over other non-Gypsies who might not share their family unity and values.

GYPSY MAGIC

During the Middle Ages, Gypsy witches and sorcerers were linked with the Romani culture and were identified with hedge witchcraft—witchcraft of the old pagan people. Like hypnotism, the Gypsy's magic must be done with the consent of the person on whom the spell would be cast, and no harm would come to that person.

According to historian and author Raymond Buckland's *Buckland's Book of Gypsy Magic*, "Gypsy magic lies in four simple ingredients: will, concentration,

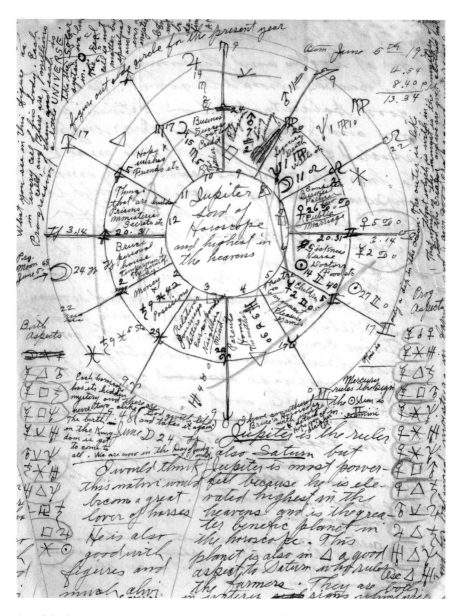

An original astronomy (horoscope) given to a client by a Gypsy fortuneteller during the 1940s. "Jupiter Lord of Horoscope and highest in the heavens."

patience, and secrecy." The proper magic takes time, and one must have patience in order to perform it correctly.

It has been said that most of the Gypsy's magical powers are performed in communion with nature outdoors. The magical powers are directly related to nature and are founded in the natural element because nature's elements have purer vibrations than non-magical or mythical powers.

THE GYPSY FORTUNETELLER

Traditionally, fortunetelling has been practiced by the women of the family. Both women and girls are properly trained in the practice of their trade. Each, however, has her own method and practice, so we will only provide a historic view on their skills.

Many fortunes are performed on the city streets, in Gypsy fortunetelling parlors, at fairs, carnivals, flea markets, in the grand hotels of the White Mountains and at other special and private events. During their travels, the Gypsies performed their fortunetelling in places where the police were unlikely to harass them and where they were not infringing on the territory of another *kumpania*.

Historian and author John Marks describes how carnival fortunetelling worked:

> *In the summer the men go out and work in carnivals, and do boiler repairing in between. They usually clear $5,000 to $6,000 for the summer after living expenses for the family, but sometimes they get only $500 to $1,000. The carnival is a big racket. They charge $25 to $200 for a fortune telling concession and then charge for lights, a watchman, and garbage. Then they tell you if there is a complaint you are on your own. In a carnival you can only make money if you steal and cheat people.*

The practice of predicting information about an individual's life is considered an art form, which is usually performed at carnivals in a Gypsy fortuneteller's parlor. They say that the scope of fortunetelling is, in principle, identical to the practice of divination. The difference is that divination is considered part of a religious ritual, while the term fortunetelling implies a less serious or formal setting, even one of popular culture, where belief in occult workings behind the prediction is less prominent than the concept of suggestion.

Historically, fortunetelling grew out of folkloristic receptions of Renaissance magic specifically associated with Gypsies. Some fortunetelling exists purely as an item of pop culture, with little or no vestiges in the occult.

It was customary for the fortuneteller to prepare herself properly in both her manner of dress and her spiritual, magical attitude. First came the costume or ritual dress, which was colorful and appropriate for this special occasion. Many wore shawls, necklaces and ornate rings.

As far as the men were concerned, they would dress in corduroy trousers of heavy cloth, with fancy horn buttons. Most often the men would adorn themselves with broad-brimmed hats and sturdy boots. On special occasions, gold jewelry was often worn by the men.

The New Hampshire Gypsy readers were most always found at carnivals, fairs, tearooms, private homes, special events and at the grand hotels in the White Mountains. At these mountain retreats, the guests would come to enjoy the solitude and peacefulness of the countryside. They would come alone or with family and spend most of the summer season; their resort was their second home. Many times they were seeking entertainment and would search out the services of a fortuneteller, a card reader, a palm reader or a crystal ball. Whatever the medium, the client wanted to be entertained. The Gypsy would convey that which she wanted her client to hear: deciphering a dream, perhaps, or revealing where the customer would travel, meet someone special or where they would find their fortune. Let us examine the methods of readings, such as the crystal ball, palm reading, the cards, astrology and other cosmic interpretation—the list goes on.

THE CRYSTAL BALL KNOWN AS THE *DUKKERING*

Typically, fortunetellers attempt to make predictions on matters such as future romantic, financial and childbearing prospects. Many fortunetellers also give "character readings." They may use numerology, palmistry and astrology if the subject is present.

According to Raymond Buckland's *Gypsy Magic*:

> Dukkering *is the common term for Rom fortunetellers, taken from the word* duk, *which means the hand or palm. Originally, this term referred only to palm reading, but it is now applied to all forms of reading. Crystal gazing has also been a popular tool for fortunetelling.*

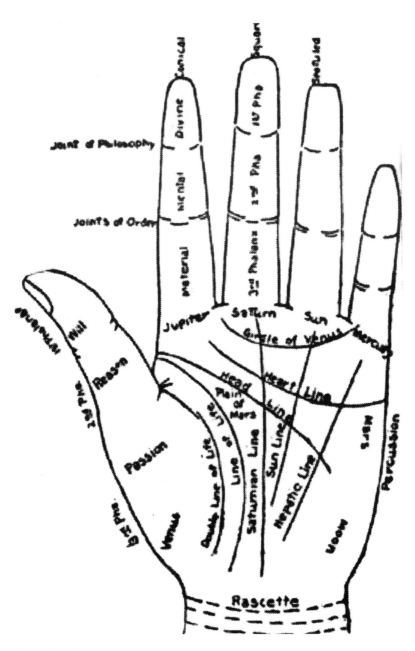

Chart of the hand.

The Gypsy fortuneteller would quietly sit at a small table in serious contemplation while gazing into his or her crystal ball. We must remember that the Gypsy and the client would learn to see what they wanted to see. Meditation was very important, as well as setting the proper atmosphere, mood and tone. A clear mind and consciousness is necessary, and then one must breathe deeply and gaze upon the crystal. The fortuneteller may see things in the crystal ball that no one else may see.

Crystal gazing is to know how to gaze. The Gypsy reader of the ball does not stare into the ball. The reader would relax and look into the crystal but would not pretend or put images in the crystal. However, if nothing happened within ten or fifteen minutes, the reader would stop and put the crystal aside and try again some other time in the near future.

Once again, the Gypsy and client would sit with the ball in front of them and wait for the proper moment in a dimly lit, quiet room. Presently, the reading would commence, and possibly a picture would appear in the crystal. What one might see would surely be symbolic, possibly a metaphor. To interpret these images may be difficult, and the reader must feel the vibrations of her client. For example, the image may be that of a lone person seen on a path in the forest, and suddenly the single path becomes two. The lone man stops, and the picture may fade away. Now was a time of reflection. What path did he take, and why? This could be interpreted as a time for decision-making—what path in life do I take? Does the client see a dream, quest or a reflection of one's own life and a problem he or she must solve? What path is the safe or challenging route?

We must remember that the Gypsy only regards the crystal ball, the cards or the palm as tools, and these tools must be treated with the utmost respect.

PALM READING

This type of reading does not rely on specific devices or methods, but rather the practitioner gives the client advice and predictions said to have come from spirits or through personal visions while examing the client's hand.

For example, the major lines of the hand are caused by the folding action of the palm. Needless to say, the physical stature and occupation of the client may determine the type of hand.

It has been said that the condition of a hand tells the reader a great deal about things like attitude, circulation, nervousness, temper, disorder, possibly rheumatism and thickness of the joints. Maybe the hand is long or short, with pointed or square fingers or with a unique shape of the nails.

According to Raymond Buckland's *Gypsy Magic*, the follow excerpts are given for palm reading:

> *Short hands: a tendency to be quick to judge. With pointed fingers judgment may be aided by imagination.*
> *Long hands: A capacity for detail and the subject will be easily satisfied. When the fingers are longer than the palm, the mind will be active.*
> *Hard hands: These show energy and perseverance. If the hand is hard and pointed, activity with elegance.*
> *Soft hands: Laziness of mind and or body. Very thick hands indicate self-esteem.*
> *There are other forms of reading, which are popular and may be used by the Romani. Some of these pertain to the physical characteristics in addition to palm reading of the client's body. Good examples would be the following:*
> *Cheeks: A serious and studious person.*
> *Chin: May indicate good luck and prosperity.*
> *Ears: Left—recklessness; the right—bravery*
> *Throat: a rich marriage*
> *Hands: Right—natural ability. Left—money problems.*
> *Hips: Strong, healthy children.*

Raymond Buckland adds other reading methods, such as reading beans; reading with a breadboard, pendulum, coins, dice and dominoes; and reading fire.

READING OF CARDS

Needless to say, Gypsies are most well known as readers of cards to indicate one's future. Today's modern playing cards are known to have come from the Minor Arcana, with designs of hearts, diamonds, spades and clubs. From the Major Arcana, the suit of cups became hearts, pentacles became diamonds, spades were taken from the swords and the clubs came from the wands. The design on the Minor Arcana cards were traditionally the kings, queens and jacks, which were all taken from the Gypsy figures. The Gypsy cards are known as tarot cards and are easily available in retail stores.

Gypsy layouts for card reading may be quite complicated. For example, Raymond Buckland tells us that "when the reader lays out the tarot cards, they choose one card that may best represent the client. This card is named as the 'significator.' Alternately, depending on the question or subject matter be discussed, different items may be used to influence the cards (spirits). A wand was likely to represent sexual feelings, and cups may be associated with love and friendship."

For further reference, I recommend *Buckland's Book of Gypsy Magic: Travelers' Stories, Stones, and Healings*, which contains spells, healings and layouts, such as the Seven Star and the Thirty Plus. A Gypsy interpretation is given with each. This *Book of Gypsy Magic* is published by the Weiser Books in San Francisco, California, 2010.

The Gypsies would often use special charms as tools for working their magic and warding off evil spirits. Most of these charms were acquired from nature. Some of the more common charms used were love beads. These natural beads were worn as necklaces, which would act as love magnets. Wearing a necklace of seeds, such as corn, acorn or sunflower seeds, is said to attract the opposite sex and ensure fertility.

Another type of charm is the love pebble. This is a small, round white stone. The stone is to be painted red with the lover's name printed on it. Ask your lover to carry it with them, and it will surely unite you as one.

There are other magical stones used as charms. They might be precious and semiprecious stones, but beware that there are many superstitions found among Gypsy families regarding these charms. Some good examples would be the following as given in *Buckland's Book of Gypsy Magic*:

Beans have been regarded as potent sexual amulets. They may be found in their pockets.

A bloodstone is known for easing childbirth, to prevent a miscarriage.

A sprinkle of cinnamon on most any food may cause amorous thoughts.

Cloves are known as fertility symbols when used as love potions.

The dog—contrary to popular belief, the dog is not man's best friend, the horse is. The dog is forbidden to enter the tent. The Gypsies' favorite breed is known as the lurcher; part greyhound and part sheepdog.

The fern seeds are often used in love potions.

The mistletoe is a century old symbol of love. A kiss beneath the mistletoe is meant to set the seal of your love.

The rabbit's foot is also known as the good luck charm.

OTHER READING

According to Raymond Buckland's *Book of Gypsy Magic*, the following are excerpts of the common methods used for fortunetelling in America:

Alectroamancy: by observation of rooster pecking at grain
Astrology: by the movements of celestial bodies
Astromancy: by the stars
Augury: by the flight of birds
Bazi or four pillars: by hour, day, month, and year of birth.
Cartomancy: card playing cards, tarot cards, or oracle cards
Cheiromancy: by the shape of the hands and lines in the palms
Chronomancy: by determination of lucky and unlucky days
Crystallomancy: by the crystal ball also called scrying
Extispicy: by the entrails of animals
Face reading: by means of variations in face and head shape
Gastromancy: by stomach-based ventriloquism (historically)
Haruspicy: by the livers of sacrificed animals
Horary astrology: the astrology of the time the question was asked
Hydromancy: by water
I Ching divination: by yarrow stalks or coins and the I Ching
Kau cim: by means of numbered bamboo sticks shaken from a tube
Lithomancy: by the stones or gems
Necromancy: by the dead, or by spirits or souls of the dead
Numerology: by numbers
Oneiromancy: by dreams
Onomancy: by names
Palmistry: by lines and mounds on the hand.

It appears that the reasons a person may consult a fortuneteller or reader are mediated by cultural expectations and by the personal desires of the client. Thus, there is no one answer as to why people consult fortunetellers.

Anne Sutherland tells us in *Gypsies: The Hidden Americans* that the *bujo*, a swindle, is very profitable. She describes the bujo as a confidence trick whereby a person (always a fortunetelling customer) is cheated out of a large savings of money. There are many ways to pull a bujo, but the most common way to pull a bujo is what the Rom (Gypsies) call in English "switch the bag," when the money is sewn up in a piece of cloth and switched for an identical bag containing cut-up newspapers. Bujo is the Romani word for bag.

History of a Nomadic Culture

Many Gypsy families toured throughout the White Mountains and claimed to have made a good living by their craft. Many families spent the summer traveling with the country fairs and carnivals, fortunetelling and operating the concessions. These readers are quite talented as storytellers; however, are they truly Gypsies or psychics, or could they be imposters?

Even though the word "Gypsies" describes persons of nomadic habits, whatever their race or origin, it does not include members of an organized group of traveling showmen or persons engaged in circuses, traveling together as such.

There were more than a dozen fairs, some state fairs, which were located throughout the White Mountain district, such as the Plymouth Fair, Sandwich Fair, Lancaster Fair, North Haverhill Fair, Lincoln Craft Fair and Cornish Fair, as well as other New Hampshire fairs not located in the White Mountains such as the Rochester Fair, Hopkinton State Fair, Stratham Fair, Cheshire Fair, Belknap County Fair, Hillborough County Fair and the Deerfield Fair. The majority of the New Hampshire fairs were agriculturally centered fairs, but they featured other entertainment and amusement for the families.

Many of the Gypsies followed the fairs and carnival circuits throughout the state where they performed their craft of fortunetelling and palm reading or working as hawkers, operators or mechanics on the midway. Being drifters and constantly traveling from one location to another, they would camp near the fairgrounds and perform whatever duties were available, such as selling carnival goods, trinkets and souvenirs or singing and dancing.

There were many grand hotels in the White Mountains that were considered popular places to perform their craft of storytelling and readings. A few of the most popular resorts were the Alpine House, the Balsams, the Crawford House, the Eagle Mountain House, Fabyan House, Franconia Inn, the Glen House, the Kearsarge House, Maplewood Hotel, the Mountain View House, Mount Pleasant House, the Mount Washington, Profile House, the Twin Mountain House and the Wentworth Hall & Cottages. These are but a few hotels and inns that may have been found throughout the White Mountains and the national park. Many have burned, been dismantled or discontinued operation. During the late nineteenth and early twentieth centuries, these summer retreats were extremely popular for the affluent city visitors.

Campsites throughout the White Mountain National Forest housed as many as nineteen first-class campgrounds. Several Gypsy families took advantage of these available campgrounds because they were accessible to their work.

Romani vardos (wagon home).

Traditionally, the men handled all the business affairs, negotiations and arrangements. They built their own booths and prepared their advertisements or handbills, and the women told the fortunes. However, if the woman's fortunetelling business was doing well and assistance was needed from members of the family, they would all contribute to her aid, including her husband, children and in-laws. Most of the members of the family would reduce their own activities in order to assist her in her business.

The skill of fortunetelling has fallen out of practice. To make money, one has to trick their audience and be on the move at all times. Many Gypsy women do not bother to tell fortunes for they don't make much money at it anymore, saying that there is no profit if you don't steal.

There are some towns that prohibit the fortuneteller from the carnival or circus, probably because the trade itself was not very lucrative unless you trick (cheat) your customer.

The Gypsies' mode of travel was the horse-drawn wagon. These Romani *vardos* were decorated elaborately with special carvings and intricate paintings in bright colors highlighted with gold leaf. There were different types of wagons, such as the Burton wagon, which were popular with Romani and showmen families. The Bush wagon was considered a standard Romani vardo, as seen in pictures in this book. Another adjunct to the wagon was the tent; they were "campers" long before modern-day campers. The entire family's one-room home was a home on wheels. These vehicles could be found throughout Europe as well as America, but it was the English wagon, known as the vardo, that was best known. The vehicle had a stove for cooking and heat, a bed and closets. Like our modern trailers, it had all the comforts of a home.

Reminiscences

In years past, Gypsies and non-Gypsy travelers provided services in the tourist trade at country resorts, hotels and amusement parks. To maintain their mobility, the Gypsies and non-Gypsies alike would avoid trades that would keep them in one location for a span of time, before or after a specific transaction. Quick, well-paid contracted jobs were highly desirable because they would enable Gypsies to work as families.

Many of the grand hotels have disappeared from the landscape, much like the horse-and-buggy, the stagecoach, the old farms and their large barns clustered about the cultivated fields and pasture land, the lumber camps throughout the White Mountains and, now, the Gypsies as we remember their colorful appearance and wagons and unique way of selling, trading and fortunetelling.

Much has been replaced with paved highways and fast automobiles, but fortunately what remains in the White Mountains are the campsites and the White Mountain National Forest, which protects the beauty of the region.

Today, there are amusement parks throughout the White Mountains, such as those listed with the White Mountain Attractions: Santa's Village, Clark's Trading Post, the Hobo Railroad, Six Gun City, Lost River and Storyland. At these parks, as well as at the grand hotels and other resorts, we will find Romanian students working during the tourist season as waitstaff, maids, bartenders, caretakers, musicians and other types of entertainment, but they are not considered Gypsies.

According to state records, many of the Gypsy descendants who live in New Hampshire also came from Ireland. During the years from 1845 to 1860, many Irish immigrants came to America due to the potato famine, and they in turn brought their myths and traveling lifestyle. However, most

Postcard of the Old Homestead, Wilton, New Hampshire.

centered in the larger communities where the textile and timber industries were located; thus, there are no recognized or unique ethnic groups of Irish travelers or Gypsies from the United Kingdom.

Today, there are several listings in the yellow pages and on websites for fortunetellers in New Hampshire, most of whom are located in the larger communities of Manchester, Dover, Rochester and Portsmouth. The White Mountain fortunetellers are well known for using tarot cards, runes and tea leaves. There are palm readers, phrenologists, psychics, numerologists and mystics. These readers are not necessarily listed as Gypsies.

This is a new age, a renaissance for magic and the ancient mysterious art of the Gypsies' craft—the crystal ball, cards and fortunetelling.

NEW HAMPSHIRE FARMLAND

The charm of the countryside is definitely represented by ancient trades, which can be gathered into symbolic museums. Archaic tools, as well as the customs and faiths related to them, have been carefully preserved by the villages along the centuries.

THE FARMER'S HOMESTEAD

As a young boy, I spent my summers on my grandparents' farm in the North Country of New Hampshire and enjoyed working with the Gypsies. I learned a great deal of their lifestyle. I especially remember watching them work the farm, listening to their music and being entertained by their dancing at the carnivals and fairs.

The Romani Gypsies told me many stories of the homeland in Romania, and now I'd like to reminisce about my own adventures living with them during the summer months.

As was stated earlier in Chapters 2 and 3, the entire Gypsy family contributes to the financial support for their existence, but it is the man of the family who is the chief and is considered the breadwinner. His duty is to support the family, and he will use any of his skills to do so. His labors, as mentioned earlier, may be as a farmer's helper, a tender of the farm animals, a peddler, a tinsmith, a worker at an iron foundry, a cooper's helper, a smithy's assistant, a "river hog" at a logging camp or even a barker at the carnival. You name it, and he will do it to the best of his ability.

Farm labor was a major source of employment for many families until automation in the field made the area of operation increasingly difficult. Most of the Gypsies' work was done during the summer. As this is only seasonal work, many of the families were unable to save enough money to live on for the off-season; therefore, they applied for welfare.

Like the Gypsies, the farmer's homestead was a tight little community; out of necessity, it was designed to be self-sufficient. As the farmer found the time from the eternal rounds of planting and harvesting, he built needed outbuildings around his dwelling. Here was where the Gypsy men entered the scene. First came the barn, with stalls for the family's cows and horses, hay wagons and perhaps a lean-to for his sheep. If, by good fortune, there was a field with a spring on the homestead, the cabin was built near it, and a springhouse became one of the outbuildings. Then came the outhouse, a smokehouse for curing meat, a root cellar, a woodshed and an ash pit. Near the barn was the corncrib, the granary, the pens for calves and hogs, a machine (tool) shed and perhaps a shop.

The buildings kept pace with the farmer's affluence. The cabin was enlarged and faced with clapboards or replaced by brick or stone and roofed with slate. The barn was replaced with a sawed lumber structure; there were many stalls for the cattle.

Postcard of a farmyard.

The timber was cleared to make new fields in the upper pasture; it was split into rails for fences and buildings. The hive of bees multiplied to a long row in the back orchard, and berry bushes lined the kitchen garden fences.

Wants and needs grew with progress. The affluent farm family was surrounded by hired hands consisting of Gypsy families. Being of an independent nature, these families did not live on the farm but rather in their own campsites near the river.

The Gypsy community exerted its own social and economic pressures on the family farm. As the spring and summer seasons dawned, their fields were no longer their islands, and their way of life was no longer under their control, for the farm chores needed tending. The neighbors were haying, and like the fields of Romania, a haystack could be sighted over in the next knoll. There the haystacks were growing like great beehives along the roadside. Some were under pointed wooden roofs, which slid up and down on huge wooden pins in their framework; others might have been uncovered. Near the high ground, the womenfolk may have been seen carrying the smaller stacks to the larger stacks.

Just down the road, about a country mile, the hired men were digging a well by slipping round tiles down through the sand until the water from the new spring arrived at the barnyard troughs. To say the least, the Gypsies were quick to learn what the farmer wanted from them.

In the same field, apple picking had begun along the roadside. Long shafts of sunlight peeked out from the orchards and painted the path that lay within them with light. The farmworkers were now brooding in nature's mystery as the long ladders were carried through the orchard bars and slid into place at the topmost branches. Some of the apples would be left until just before a cold snap, which would color them and sweeten their flavor. One old hand commented, "Let 'em hang for dew and sun." Damn, they talk strange.

In the west pasture, the heifers were being driven down for the slaughter. Even the sheep were brought closer to the shelter of the farm buildings. The farmer-butcher had waited for cold weather so that the meat would not spoil. As the hired men watched, the water was steaming up above the pot, and all was ready. They had never seen anything like that before—the curved wooden gambrels laid on the wall waiting to have the massive forms hung upon them like coats in the back shed. All the men hurried to witness the slaughter but did not outdistance the final pleading of these barn creatures and did not witness the final event.

To pass some time, the *Rom baro* Gypsy and his men could not help but notice the smartweed growing wild by the snake fence near the brook. *Glata*, young boys, sat by the brook and watched the trout, dreaming of buckshot, sinkers, cork dobbers and hickory poles. Down by the swim hole, young voices could be heard, and from the naked form balancing in the soft light on the mossy log was decreed, "If ma says it's so, then it's so."

CLEARING THE LAND

We must remember that the Romani Gypsies work hard and wish to satisfy the boss. But they will remind the owner of the farm that their work is only seasonal and they are to be left alone and receive their pay regularly and they will do good work. The Gypsies have strong work ethics, as we have already mentioned; however, they bear watching.

The only work that paid anything worthwhile was farming (clearing the land, tending the cattle and general labor). It was not easy work being in the hot sun all day, but they did not have to mix with the non-Gypsies. They did not have to eat and board at the farm—they were content.

Here in the North Country, there are two seasons of harvest. The first season encompasses the gathering of grain and fruit in the fall, and the second season of harvest is in the spring, when the product is the ubiquitous stones piled throughout the pasture. What the farmland grows well is granite.

Postcard of hay making at Whitefield, New Hampshire.

Postcard of a wheat harvest.

History of a Nomadic Culture

Picking stones was a regular task on the farm, with a steady income. Many farmers felt it was the surest crop of the year, never affected by rain, drought, blizzard or heat. Religiously each spring, the field that was reasonably clear last season yielded a new abundant harvest. Such is the power and will of Mother Nature as she unlocks the frozen earth each spring. The Gypsies don't really mind the work, but the Americans were lazy.

The farmer has developed various techniques for reaping this annual harvest. One technique was to use a dump cart and throw the rocks into it as the horses plodded slowly over the ground that was recently turned into ribbons of moist brown. Another was the efficient use of the stone boat so that weight could be transferred on a more horizontal plane. The third technique consisted of the stones being tossed into piles before they were transferred to a conveyor. With these stones, boundary lines of the property were built—thus, the stone wall.

After the land has been cleared of this harvest of granite, simple tools to cultivate the land or the newly expanding field played a major role. The axe, hoe, spade, shovel, horse and plow were the basic tools that helped develop the fields.

There are degrees of honor among farm shovels, but the farmer's pride is a long-handled, sharp-pointed one. The hired help were expected to use the tools provided. Hands were used for digging postholes and for bringing loads of gravel for the farm drive. The prized shovels were kept in the tool shed, oiled and kept clean. The young workers were never allowed to use them, for a good farmer knew that when a man had a tool that just fit his hands, such a tool must be cherished and cared for.

The owner of the farm would remind his hired men that there is plowing and there is plowing. In a field studded with stones, seen and unseen, plowing became a sort of wrestling match, with the odds favoring Mother Nature. When the share strikes a hidden stone, the chain connecting the clevis to the whiffle tree slackens. And, because of some mysterious law of physics, the handles jump up and catch a man under the ribs. At such a moment, a local farmer knew why some of his ancestors didn't look back at the upland pastures.

Plowing in the fall was good work for it gave a man a chance to hear the blue jays screaming in the beeches and the crows calling from the maple grove in the south pasture. While the team was taking a break, one could hear the chickadees in the gray birches on the other side of the upland pasture walls. As the Gypsies lifted their eyes to the hills across the valley, they could see the brown of the oak leaves blending with the

Cattle tending.

green of the pines and the hemlocks that reminded them all of how glad they were that they came to this country to work and wander through the mountains.

Farm labor was considered a major source of their income. Most Gypsy families still do farm labor during the summer months. When families are engaged in farm labor year-round, they usually camp in the field or stay in fruit shacks provided by the employer. This was where a man's eye could rise to witness the beauty of the White Hills.

CATTLE TENDING

Another Gypsy chore was to tend the cattle. On the lighter side, it was especially interesting to watch the young folk witness the Jerseys, Guernseys, Durhams and Holsteins all come running for their salt. As they lapped the salt with their rough tongues, the men looked them over with judicious eyes, comparing notes on breeds and animals. Romanians had to learn quickly the differences among the cattle. Good farmers knew their cattle, and you might have heard them comment, "The eye of the master fatteneth the floch."

As the sun lowered itself behind the upland pasture, our group, including myself, moved slowly down the boulder road toward home and their evening chores. The cattle drifted toward the spring and their supper's grazing. All seemed well in the highland pasture. The stock had been salted again.

It was time for the cows to return home and time once again for the daily ritual of milking. When one sits on an old three-legged stool, as

Tin peddler.

they used on the country farm, close to the smooth, warm flank, with a ten-quart pail between his knees, there is a restful rhythm as the jet of milk shoots downward with a regular but steady force. The first few streams of milk played a tune on the metal containers, and at the end of the flow, the music came to a close. The white lines sunk into a rounded mass of bubbly froth.

Milking time was considered very restful, provided that Bossy had been sprayed in order to keep the flies away and that she had a crib full of green oats or the tops of sweet corn on which to munch. A good farmer treated his cattle very gently so that he didn't have to worry about the cow kicking his pail or becoming unruly.

Milking wasn't the best job on the farm, but it was far from the worst. The Gypsies and I cleaned the barn, laying a fresh layer of sawdust to cover the gutters and floors. With the cows chewing noisily, two or three cats waiting for supper and the farm dog watching with a guardian eye, the farmer felt a sense of well-being. He was content and said to his farmhands, "Well done, men. You may return to your family campsite. Don't be late tomorrow."

GYPSY PEDDLERS

The Hucksters

The peddler's wagon traveled from town to town and, at one time, linked American farms to the crossroads of the country village. The metaphysical superstore contained all the traditional tools of the craft. Here they carried and sold all the standard items and household goods, including tinware, trinkets, clothes and sundries of novelties made by the Gypsies. A lot of these pagan wares were made with strict attention to detail and the proper correspondence to assure their magical value. These traders were very active during the early 1900s. Many of the wagons were horse-drawn piloted by the rugged, versatile Gypsies who were more than peddlers; they were an institution, a cog in the wheel of progress. The roads they traveled were either ankle-deep in dust or knee-deep in mud. Through heat and cold, the faithful Gypsies made their rounds. This peddling business was most likely a family affair and was resourceful and hardy.

The night before, they would have stocked the shelves of the wagon and filled the special orders from the previous trip. The wagon jolted out before dawn and drove into the countryside with the prospects and hopes of making more sales.

The peddler's wagon was a light-wheeled rig, either with roll-up canvas or wood sides, which supported shelving. Two horses were used to pull the wagon, which was light enough to make good speed.

Later, during the early twentieth century, the auto trucks came into being. The days of peddling were numbered; the tempo of country life quickened, and their business withered on the vine.

The Country Tinsmith

If it wasn't for the tinware industry, the country peddler would not have reached the popularity it did, and the Gypsies knew it. This craft had its rise in New England, but the Gypsy was well versed in the craft from the English in Europe. Edward and William Pattison began making culinary vessels in the small town of Berlin. Much of the supply of tin came from Ireland and England, and they were soon turning out a variety of household utilities. They are rightfully considered the first makers of tinware in America.

It was in Ireland and England that many Gypsies lived and worked, and they mastered the trade that was entirely fabricated by hand. The tin sheets were thin plates of charcoal-smelted iron, which had been reduced in a rolling mill and then coated with melted tin. The coating process consisted of three dips for what was called single tinplates, six for durable tinplate.

The tin produced such utensils as pans, pails, plates, teapots, coffeepots, bake ovens, cups and measurers. As mentioned earlier, this was the perfect product for the peddler to make his living.

We must remember that these pieces were not produced for the luxury market but were produced in quantity for popular sale by the peddler or the local country store. The primitive designs used by the local artisans were often more interesting than those of the more highly commercialized competitors of the time.

Another form of decoration the artisan used was the pinprick or punched work. This style consisted of raised or embossed designs made by tapping a blunt instrument with a hammer in order to dent the tin but not pierce it completely.

Postcard of Basil's Blacksmith Shop.

Postcard of the interior of blacksmith shop.

It is said that the commonest of all lighting devices made by the tinsmith was the lantern, which for many years was of the traditional Paul Revere type: a cylinder of tin with holes pierced in the sides and a peaked top with a ring handle. Other lanterns included the candle boxes, tinderboxes and matchboxes. Tin lamps were extremely common before glass lanterns appeared on the kitchen shelf. These items were possibly the most popular items sold by the Gypsy peddlers.

Another very popular tin piece was the foot warmer. This item had a wooden frame and handle and was used in the meetinghouse on the Sabbath and in the family sleigh on weekends. Many of these portable stoves have survived and may be found in local taverns and country homes today.

The Village Smithy

The old-time blacksmith was considered a mechanic of no mean ability. It was not unusual for the male Gypsy to help the blacksmith, for they were known for their ability as skilled ironworkers and tinsmiths. The blacksmith shop was considered a horse-trading center of the community, the clearinghouse for farm gossip and labor. There the inevitable town bums of the community had their hangout. There the village fool paraded his ignorance, the village wit traded his lewd banter and the young bloods boasted about the speed of their horses or their girls.

The shop kept all senses alert. There was a sooty forge, with sparks that flew from glowing metal under the hammer, the ring of the anvil and the pungent odor of a burning hoof under the heat of the hot horseshoe. There was the hiss of steam from the tub of water used for cooling hot shoes and the sharp animal smell of a sweaty horse; the blacksmith himself, with his bulging muscles, his hands so careless of the heat of a hot shoe; and the pile of old iron, buggy wheel and wagon wheel rims, worn-out horseshoes, metal parts of this and that. Stomping at flies in the shade of a nearby tree were horses waiting their turn.

The clientele of the blacksmith shop was strictly stag. To the men of the rural community, it was a truly masculine, comfortable, satisfying place—the Gypsy men were in their glory.

The Cooper's Shop

Just ask the average youngsters today what was made in a cooper shop, and chances are they don't know. Yet in certain old New England towns, more common than the village smithy was the farm cooper shop, where wooden barrels were made by hand.

Most of the early mountain settlers had to learn many skills for survival; being a cooper was one such skill. This was not very different for the Gypsies, for when they came to the North Country they were well equipped with such skills and ready for the task set before them.

As time passed, small shops appeared on the scene, most of which were near lumber mills, well equipped with a workbench, a few simple tools, a frame for setting up barrels and a fireplace. The lumber they used came from the nearby sawmills. During the nineteenth and early twentieth centuries, the great abundance of good quality oak and chestnut timber led many of the citizens of the town to engage in the manufacture of barrels and other casks. Later, oak and chestnut thinned out and white pine was used instead. It was not difficult to find labor, as many seasonal men, generally Gypsies, were available to do the work, even for lower pay.

Forest trees to be converted to lumber for barrels were marked, felled and later cut in the forest into bolts the right length for staves. In the mill, these bolts were sawed into staves by the cylindrical barrel-saw. From other bolts the required size, barrel heads were cut and beveled, either in one piece or for some casks in several pieces.

Wooden hoops for the barrels were made from gray birch saplings an inch or two in diameter, sometimes from alder or maple. Cut to approximately the right length, with the bark left on and split in two lengthwise, they were delivered to the shop tied in bunches to be thrown into tanks containing water to soak until pliable enough to form the hoops.

Many Gypsies rarely spent the winter months in the woods. Rather, they would move on to work indoors with the cooper or other craftsmen; thus, some farmers spent that time preparing hoops instead of setting up barrels. (We must remember they are a traveling group of people, and they wander to different jobs.) Now the farmer must cut their saplings, split them, shave them to the right thickness and tie them together for delivery to the larger shops. Many times you would recognize these shops or farms, as the staves and heading were piled outside for seasoning.

Franconia Mountains and stone iron furnace.

Once the lumber was seasoned, the cooper and his men would trim the staves, setting aside a shaving horse, which held the staves. It took a skilled cooper to shape a stave for a tight barrel. His work had to be accurate so that the finished barrel would be symmetrical. Only careful work accomplished this end, but the experienced cooper could turn out staves so uniform that no further fitting was necessary when put together in barrel shape. That was no problem for the Gypsies, as they knew what they were doing.

Next came setting up the barrel. In a form the size of the required cask or keg, the staves were set upright. A rope was put around the staves and was tightened by a windlass to draw them together, and temporary iron hoops were fitted over the top and bottom to hold them in place.

Now it was time for the firing. A cylindrical cresset, smaller in diameter than the barrel and open at both ends, stood in the fireplace. Inside this a fire was built. Over the barrel they slipped and heated the staves to shrink the fibers and set them in shape. The fired barrel was returned to the form to be tightened again. It was now ready for permanent hoops.

The birch saplings were taken from the tanks, their ends tapered a little and cut to fit the casks. Shaved to the right thickness and the ends notched, the hoops could be clamped together by means of the notches.

The first hoops adjusted were bilge hoops, one on either side of the swelling of the barrel. Quarter hoops were often used midway between the bilge and the ends of the barrel. After fitting, they were tapped gently into place with a wedge-shaped hoop and driven in place with the cooper's hammer. The tap-tap of the hammer was a customary sound heard from the shop.

Next, the stave ends were beveled, the chime or rim smoothed and the groove for the heads cut. Once the kegs were complete, they were immediately put into service. These were carefully piled on wagons with a tall, wide rigging attached and sent to the nearest depot for shipment to the coastal cities of Portsmouth, Boston, Providence, Pawtucket, New York and Philadelphia. Some of the charm of the old villages has vanished as the Gypsies have traveled on to new pastures, and the musical tap-tap of the cooper's hammer is no longer heard.

The Iron Foundry

The mountain had a need for cooking utensils, nails, firearms and other hardware such as latches and hinges, so iron foundries dotted the landscape. Of course, we don't think of New Hampshire as being the source of iron, but here in the Granite State, foundries were established and ran at a profit for several years.

In Franconia, New Hampshire, an inventor from Massachusetts established an iron foundry. The foundry was located just a few miles north of the Old Man of the Mountain in Franconia Notch. Here it smelted a rich vein of ore, possibly the richest bed of ore known at that time. This bed consisted of a wall of iron running deep into the nearby hillside.

The iron furnace is located beside the river in Franconia. Behind the tower, there are traces of the road down the embankment where the ore was hauled from Iron Mountain, or Ore Hill, as it was called during the 1800s.

As soon as the ore was collected, it was immediately brought to the village or blacksmith forge. Hand-driven bellows or water wheels blew air into the crucible filled with lime, charcoal and the iron ore. The heat of the burning charcoal melted the ore, and the lime acted as a flux as it rose to the top of the molten mass. Once this "doss" was skimmed off, the layer below was left as pure iron.

At this point, the iron maker could pour this molten iron into sand molds to make "hollow ware," as household utensils were then called, or rectangular

Postcard of the freight yard in Warner, New Hampshire.

plates, referred to as "fire backs," that were mounted in the fireplaces to retain the heat.

Beginning in 1811, the company employed ten men to blast out the ore and transport it downhill to the blast furnace. Production grew steadily to the point where the foundry needed more men to produce finish items such as nails, kettles and sundry tools. At the height of production, the company employed more than fifty men on a yearly basis and another fifty when the large furnace was actually in full blast.

John Spargo's *Iron Mining and Smelting in Bennington, Vermont 1786–1842*, provides the following description:

> *Generally, the autumn and winter months are chosen to put the furnace in blast, the workmen then being obtained at lower wages (as there was no competition for farm labor this time of year) and the outdoor workmen being called in. It has been ascertained, also, that a larger quantity of iron is reduced, in a given time, in the winter months, which is supposed to be dependent on the more condensed and drier state of the atmosphere, by which the nature of the blast is modified; while the draught if the furnace is also affected by the heating gases and the surrounding air.*

This did not bother our labor force. However, despite the high quality it produced, the Franconia furnace simply could not compete with the more accessible furnaces south, where better transportation was provided them. Gradually, the labor force was reduced, and eventually the Franconia foundry closed its doors.

The local forges have vanished, and the only remains are the small dam sites and spillways that powered the water wheels. Now, the roar of the furnace, the pounding of machinery and the belching smoke is no longer visible in the mountains. Our memory lingers on, our legacy established, but the epitaph is written.

LOGGING IN THE WHITE MOUNTAINS

With the arrival of the railroad came the logging industry to the White Mountain slopes, thus changing the climate and clientele of what was once farming land.

According to *The White Mountain National Forest's Waterville Unit Plan, 1978*, "There were more lumbermen than agriculturists, and many farmers had their own sawmills, relying heavily on logging and lumbering to survive on their rocky lands." During this period, the logging industry depended primarily on the waterways of the Pemigewasset and Mad Rivers.

According to the *Waterville Unit Plan*:

> *Starting about 1850, as the farms were being abandoned for the richer farmlands of the mid-west, forest lands in the Valley were bought up in very large tracts by land companies and trusts such as the Merrimack River Lumber Company and the New Hampshire Land Company. Extensive logging operations started about 1880 and continued for fifty years.*

Francis Belcher, in his *Logging Railroads of the White Mountains*, wrote, "Official State and Federal Government reports show that lumber production in New Hampshire tripled from the late 1860's to 1900, finally reaching an all-time high of 650 million board feet in 1907. But the production then dwindled rapidly and never again challenged the records set in 1895 to 1907."

In Waterville Valley, large-scale logging operations commenced during the 1880s under such companies and landholdings as the White Mountain Paper Co., the Publishers Paper Company, the International Paper Company and the Parker Young Company.

Postcard of the Old Mill, North Woodstock, New Hampshire.

By the 1890s, the *Waterville Unit Plan* had reported about the railroads:

> *An extensive network of logging railroads were built in Thornton Gore.*
> *The present Tripoli Road runs close to the main railroad grade there.*
> *Sawmills were located in Lincoln, Woodstock, and Beebe River. Many*
> *of the old roadbeds developed into the current trail system. Most of this*
> *logging was for spruce, which was stored in piles below the driving dams*
> *in the winter and then driven down during the spring run-off...As late*
> *as 1915, the best spruce was picked out for ship spars. The rest went for*
> *lumber or pulpwood.*

The early lumberjacks and rivermen were a special breed: wanderers, drifters and Gypsies. In order to maintain their mobility, the Gypsies avoided any trade that would bind them in time to specific transactions. Many of them, being seasonal laborers, lived apart from the non-Gypsies, for they lived in their trailers and wagons in the forests and on the rivers of the North Country, like the Pemigewasset, Mad and Baker Rivers. When there was a convenient campground, they stayed there. They were a product of the time and their environment, but now this has passed and they no longer exist.

River hogs.

Grace H. Bean's *The Town at the End of the Road: A History of Waterville Valley* notes the drama of logging, saying:

> *From the 1880's up to 1930, the life of the lumberjacks was rough, dangerous, often spectacular, requiring skill and physical hardiness. The log drives down the river, for example, with their excitement, confusion, and noise, are unforgettable. Individual dramas, too, gave an edge to the logger's daily life, which sometimes ended in tragedy, sometimes made buddies out of strangers.*
>
> *They are thinly clad, for heavy clothes would be an impediment to their work. Contrary to one's idea of these hired woodsmen, they do not appear robust; many of them are of dark skin, hollow-cheeked, and possibly sunken chests. However, some Eastern Europeans are rather stocky.*

A Drama of the River Hogs

It all started where countless streams and rivers came tumbling down the remote mountains. There were no roads suitable for transporting the logs to the mills, so the only reasonable way to get the logs out of the dense forests was by the rivers. As the early cowboy drove his cattle, so the "river hogs" drove the logs when the melting snows swelled the rivers.

The river hogs were born, borrowed, but not made. As early as eight years of age, they began practicing with the pike pole and the peavey, working first in the still waters of the millponds and later on the log drive. These men developed an unarticulated love of and respect for the river. The work was hard and dangerous, the food was not the best, there were no women and wages were very low, yet the call of the river drew them, just as the frontier cowboy was called to the open prairie. To the Gypsies, it was a good job; for them, it paid well.

The business of the river man was to guide (drive) the logs from the rollways alongside the streams, where the lumberjacks had piled them during the winter months, to the sawmills downriver. The drive might last three weeks or as long as two years if the water was low and the logs became stranded on dry ledges. A river man spent most of his time lugging and prying, lifting the heavy, inert timbers from where they were jammed against the bank and shoving them out into the moving water.

Log driving was a special skill, and that didn't mean just standing on the log without falling off or being able to ride it in quiet water. You only have to tell a Rom what to do, and it would be done. Riding a log in quiet water and riding it in fast water required two different sets of muscles and reflexes. A trip down the river was a very simple task, for a man merely stepped on a log, stuck his peavey into it and leaned on the handle while the river's current swept him away. But if the water was rough, he used the peavey as a balancing pole. If another log came along to roll him under, he just stepped onto the new log and continued his ride.

Quick judgment, endurance, physical strength and balance constituted the essential skills needed to be an expert river hog. There was, however, one more essential quality for the river hog's "log sense": experience. The tendencies of currents, the effect of the water's volume and swiftness, the places where jams are likely to occur, how to avoid pile-ups, where they would break, the probable situation of the key log, rollway-breaking, dam-running, etc.—all of these experiences marked the river man who rose to the top of his profession. There were many local men who toiled to be river hogs, but they were soon replaced by good Roms.

The advent of the railroads in the 1840s brought a great change to the landscape of our north woods. A vast new territory was opened for lumbering, primarily in the wilderness of the Pemigewasset Valley, to meet the needs of a rapidly growing nation. To the lumbermen and the railroad companies, this was good seasonal job security, and the Gypsies loved it.

Unfortunately, through careless methods of cutting, the early settlers and loggers removed large portions of the virgin timber in the valley and slopes throughout the notches of the White Mountains. By their selection of the valuable conifers—the spruce, white pine, hemlock and balsam—of which the primeval forest was mostly composed, they brought about a great change in the general character of the Pemigewasset Valley. So comparatively small was the ratio of the amount of timber cut to the vast forestland available, and so considerable was the reproduction on the cutting over land originally cleared for pasture and agricultural purposes but subsequently abandoned as unprofitable, that no apprehension of the region being sometime in the future denuded of its forest covering came into the minds of lovers of the Franconia Notch during the earlier period of its use and growth as a summer and winter vacation resort area.

Driving through the wooded countryside of the Notch today, we may see evidence of the widespread cutting of timberland. Apart from the long history of extensive cutting, the forest shows the marks of repeated burning. In the early days of clear-cut logging, tops and trimmings (in loggers' parlance) were simply left where they fell. There were no cleanup duties—cut 'em and leave 'em.

History of a Nomadic Culture

In 1867, the State of New Hampshire owned the greater part of the White Mountain region. However, the policy of the state was to dispose of its public lands as fast as possible, which led to large tracts of land being sold for almost nothing.

Around the turn of the century, the logging contractors began replacing the horse and oxen with steam-powered movers. The first and possibly the most famous of these was the Lombard log hauler. With this new technology of lumbering in the North Country, the logging companies began laying out logging railroads in order to carry their lumber to the river for the drive. Sometimes they railed them all the way to the mills in North Woodstock.

New owners of this rich domain were speculators who cut off as rapidly as they could all the mature timber in order to pay the taxes and obtain as much profit as possible. At length, the increasing scarcity of spruce timber and the tariff on building materials impelled the owners to cut the trees below the line of their maturity. These considerations, leading to destructive cutting, were strongly reinforced by the further inducement arising from the demands of the wood-pulp industry, which caused some owners to cut off the trees entirely. This was true especially in places such as the higher slopes in the notches where logging was difficult. In many cases, a quarter of a century or more was required to restore the forest; in others, fires often ran over the denuded area, not only consuming all vegetation but also leading the land to be lost to forest production. Unfortunately, the aim of the lumbermen was evidently to wrest the last dollar from the land. In the process, every valuable timber area was either bought by the large lumber and paper companies or, when still held by the original owners, was subject to contracts, which called for the cutting of the trees under certain conditions of stumpage.

The romance, however, is still quite vivid among the old-timers of the North Country. The loggers have gone and the Gypsies have traveled on, but the mills remain on the rocky banks of the tributaries to the Pemigewasset. They are checkered about the landscape as battle scars, though picturesque in their romance of usefulness. From Cannon Mountain tramway has gone forth much of the lumber that was used in the homes of the Pemigewasset Valley.

Time was that this picturesque valley was more populated than it is today. There were more farms and laborers of the forest cutting and drawing from the landscape for their livelihood. Now, the cycle has returned to the appreciation of what Mother Nature intended for us: the majesty and grandeur of the forest, mountains and waterways.

Chapter 4

VACATION IN THE MOUNTAINS

FAIR TIME IN NEW HAMPSHIRE

Plymouth State Fair: A Gypsy Narrative

While I spent several spring seasons teaching American history at the Babes-Bolyai University in Cluj-Napoca, Romania, many of the following stories were recounted to me in my research of Gypsy culture and their ways in America. This particular story of the Plymouth State Fair was related to me by a Gypsy friend of mine by the name of Calin Giurgiu, from Romania, who reminisced about his grandfather's experience while their family lived and worked in the White Mountains.
Calin himself came over to the White Mountains and worked at Santa's Village during the summer seasons of 2003–04. This story, while basically true, is the author's interpretation and rendering of Calin's story.

The Gypsies chose the Plymouth Fair for their family outing. The fair was the closest to their mountain camp near the logging camp in North Woodstock on the Pemigewasset. With one horse and their camping trailer, the family was on its way to be entertained instead of entertaining. They did, however, want to see how the fairs compared with other American carnivals.

Pemigewasset Valley and Franconia Mountains.

Postcard of the Woodstock Lumber Company, Woodstock, New Hampshire.

Postcard view from Mount Agassiz Stove, looking toward the Franconia Valley, White Mountains.

It was a beautiful September day, the sun rising in a slight haze on the far eastern view, and the air was chilled by an early morning frost. Morning chores about the campsite were hurried with the excitement of the forthcoming day, and by 7:30 a.m., the horse was hitched and ready to travel. An ample lunch was packed in the round wooden butter boxes stored under the seats, and the family was ready to travel.

The horse trotted rhythmically down the mountain road. Autumn had not begun. Along the roadside were the purple flowers, and the air was sweet with the aroma of wild grapes.

As they approached the fairgrounds, they saw that there were many strangers there. On all the roads and crossroads, buggies, democrats, carryalls and farm wagons were all going to the fair; even the Gypsies' horse seemed to catch the excitement and trotted briskly along the level way. Soon the fairgrounds came into view, with the open pasture land and the big exhibition tents clearly visible. The family arrived at the main gate with their brightly colored wagon and was greeted by a polite gentleman who directed them to the parking space where the vendors were located near the midway—he thought that the family was a vendor and let them in with no charge.

With a stream of other vehicles, they went directly into the grounds and found a place near the display tents and sideshows. Their horse was unhitched

Midway fairgrounds. *Courtesy of R.J. McGinnis.*

from the wagon and planted well within display of the other vendors on the strip. It was then, at a little past ten o'clock in the morning, that without any hesitation, the family assumed their role as vendors by adorning the appropriate costume of the colorful fortuneteller (*drabarimos*). In front of the wagon they set up the fortuneteller's parlor (*ofisa*), well equipped with the crystal ball, of course. Nobody questioned them, so the husband became the hawker for the concession. The children were directed to scout through the fairgrounds for any loose change they could find on the ground.

Here were the wonders they had come to see—the awesome mystery of the sideshow tents. The attendant placed the Gypsy family right next to the palm reader, and of course, there was the Wild Man from Borneo and the girlie show nearby.

Outside the tents, there were barkers selling their wares for the show, strange-looking men dressed in very strange clothes. Walking beside the display tents was exciting enough without going inside the tent; it was like being in some far-off land found in a geography book. At one tent, glittering brass cymbals flashed in the sunlight, while at another, tambourines jangled in the hands of a dancer.

Prizewinning cattle at the fairgrounds. *Courtesy of R.J. McGinnis.*

The fair was an agricultural event where the local farmers would display their goods in the neatly clustered display tents. Here, each tent was well labeled for the exhibited crafts, food and farm animals. In the fields was the horse- and ox-pulling contests. For the amusement of the young people, there was a midway.

There was time for the family to roam the grounds, so they strolled over to the livestock stables to view the hogs, hens, horses and oxen.

Mother insisted that they go to the exhibition tent and see the prize quilts and rugs. Some of these quilts were made of tiny squares, while others were like flower gardens. With the quilts were many rugs—braided, crocheted and hooked. How many hours of patient work went into their making! Long winter hours in the farm kitchen when the road was piled with snow, long winter evenings with the kerosene lamp on the pine table; Father reading *Leavitt's Almanac*, the children playing dominoes and Mother sewing patchwork. And now the quilts and rugs were proudly displayed at the fair.

Around the display tents were showcases of glittering cheap jewelry, beads and pins and tables of souvenir knickknacks, little fluted vases and

Gypsy cookout.

small cups and pin trays with "State Fair" stamped on them. From the main exhibit tent, they wandered on to the displays of home-canned pickles, fruit and jelly. There were large delicious-smelling apples, red and green, and all kinds of vegetables, huge yellow pumpkins and mammoth squashes. Here they left the great hall and joined Father to look at the cattle in the long sheds, then to the poultry house to see the pert highbred roosters and hens, White Leghorns, Plymouth Rocks, Buff Cochins, sprightly gamecocks and diminutive bantams.

Presently, it was noon. The family and friends returned to the wagon, prepared the fire pit for hot dogs and other meats and enjoyed the homemade bread and butter pickles, cold roast chicken, pumpkin pie, chocolate frosted cake and big molasses cookies they had brought with them. After lunch and good conversation, the group returned to their tent. There was no rest for the weary as customers passed by the wagon, wishing to have their fortunes told and asking many questions like: Where are you from? What do you do? Why are you dressed strangely? The questions never ended.

After entertaining the visitors, the family leisurely strolled around the grounds. An amusing sight for the family was the organ grinder, a small dark-

Wagons and democrats. *Courtesy of R.J. McGinnis.*

skinned man with a big mustache. Then there was a man selling balloons and little whips. Father bought some red balloons and tiny horsewhips for his boys. From the peanut vendor, he bought a multicolored bag of peanuts in their shells; they were still very warm from the roaster.

Shortly after lunch, the grand street parade began with prancing horses, cattle of every description, the smart-sounding town bands, a colorful school float, the grange and church floats and old fancy democrats polished to the tee. What a grand parade!

It was now time for the family to hitch up the horse and make their departure. With wonder, they watched the visitors in their fancy democrats leave the fairgrounds. As the family and others streamed away from the fairgrounds, the road was filled with buggies and wagons. As the family approached the crossroad in the village, many took the south road while the Gypsy family traveled north to Woodstock, where their camp was located near their place of work, the Woodstock Lumber Company.

Later, only two wagons were in sight. How quiet the mountain road seemed as the horse slowly climbed the last long hill in the twilight of the shortening autumn day. In the distance, Cannon Mountain could be seen. The family arrived back at their campsite soon after dark.

Note: Yes, the vendors are still barking their wares, and the fine exhibits may still be seen, as well as the cattle-pulling contests. The Plymouth Fair is one of the oldest fairs in the state and is still a tradition in New Hampshire. It's a fine place to reminisce and meet new friends.

MOUNTAIN MEMORIES

This true story is based on a Romani family vacation in the White Mountains, which was related to me by Paul Iarcas, a Romanian friend of mine. Because of the nature of the story, I couldn't resist embellishing on this narrative for the reader.

It was during the early 1940s when the Gypsy family and their friends were preparing the camp and setting themselves for the adventurous hike in the White Mountains.

There had been a time, remembered with some pride, when the Gypsies had done a fair amount of tramping in the mountains. Accordingly, there flashed through their minds vistas from mountain peaks, the feeling of cold brook water and the sounds of friendly nights from the campsite near the ridge of these hills. It soon appeared, however, that a mountain climb was not part of this recollection. Such pleasures they considered only for goofers, and they were not.

"Climbers," Father informed the group, "were divided into four categories: goofers, peakbaggers, backpackers and pros. *Goofers* are considered the

History of a Nomadic Culture

Postcard from Dolly Copp Campgrounds, Pinkham Notch, New Hampshire.

lowest form of human life and are not experienced climbers. They would be identified mostly by the fact that they eat and sleep in camps or makeshift huts where they were served by others for a fee. They try to climb as many peaks as possible, to cover as many trails as possible or to climb a particular trail as many times as possible.

"Above *peakbaggers* are the *backpackers*. These are known as thrifty, hardworking, energetic people who shun the help of others and carry with them whatever food, clothing and bedding they deem necessary for survival in the wilderness.

"Lastly, are the *pros*. These are the men who clear the trails and who, when needed, rescue the goofers, who are lost, caught in a storm or otherwise in trouble."

With this enlightenment about climbing, the group considered doing a double-take and a reverse twist and considered lightly packed, hot meals prepared by others. What we should do, Father informed them, is to backpack into the Great Gulf Wilderness (Mount Washington) and there live in an open three-sided shelter, which could easily be made by them.

Mountain trails come in many sizes and conditions, and the Great Gulf Trail probably was the most highly developed of trails. Carefully graded with a slight but steady pitch, it seemed almost straight for several miles. Most trails are cut out of the Great Gulf Wilderness for the purpose of climbers like this group. On these there is no grading of any kind; after small trees have been cut out to show the way, they are so high that they make walking uncomfortable. Occasionally, trails follow up mountain slides that were created by an avalanche of trees and rocks in especially soggy springs. These trails, like the trails above the timberline, are marked, possibly by spotted paint. It was a pleasant walk for the Gypsy group as they enjoyed the calmness of the forest and the music of the birds. They noticed how the air and water were constantly changing the rocks and trees.

Upon returning to camp that night, supper was being prepared over a wood fire, and as the sun dropped below the mountain ridge, the Gypsies found, to their surprise, that they were soon in their sleeping gear and quite seriously ready to go to sleep.

It was noticeable that few slept peacefully, for some of the family had difficulty becoming accustomed to the roar of the nearby brook; the rustling in the fir balsams that sounded so much like an oncoming rain; the tantalizing hum of mosquitoes and common flies; and the scratching of porcupines, chipmunks, raccoons and the tiny birds that resented the intrusion into an area so plainly theirs. The object was to ignore these distractions to sleep.

The next morning, the group set off without packs, except lunch. Their object was a trip along the Glen Road in the Presidential Range. It appeared modest among mountains of great height, with no established trail to the summit. Later, the group agreed it was a mountain that had much to be modest about. It was ascended by climbing a treacherous rockslide, and its summit was covered with trees foreclosing all but the most limited views. The entire group could not imagine anyone climbing this mountain for any reason other than the record.

Father, of course, was the first to ascend, and all noticed how he puffed and perspired all the way up. Needless to say, when they returned to the shelter, Father seemed somewhat concerned. "Tomorrow," he said, "we are going to carry our packs through the Carter Notch and then climb Wildcat Mountain. But after today, without a pack and all, I think it would be better if we tried to go down to the Thompson Falls. We could again leave our packs and climb from there." It was plain to see that he was faithful to the concept of backpacking, but many in the group had begun to quail at the prospect of uninterrupted wilderness and were ready to admit defeat; others in the group were goofers and peakbaggers at heart.

The Gypsies made their way through the nearby notch. They all arrived safely in the afternoon at a shelter at the Dolly Copp Campgrounds. Taking

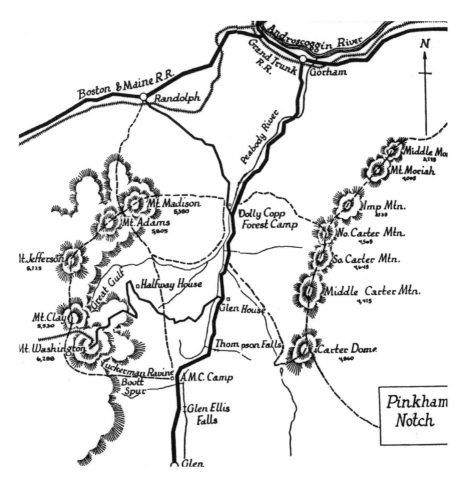

Pinkham Notch map.

a late swim in the cold mountain water, the group gathered together in the sun and freely bathed themselves, as they felt fully cut off from the world by the high cliffs of the nearby mountains.

For some families, walking in the open air is a sufficient diversion in itself. Others require an additional occupation, such as looking for birds or flowers, taking or painting pictures, hunting or fishing. Many of these travelers and campers seem to return to the mountains and their favorite places to set up the camp because in the mountains there is the challenge of nature. For the Gypsies, the mountains also say something to the soul. They beckon us home.

Before the soul reaches the place where it finally yields, it needs to refresh and nourish much of the body in which it resides. But the refreshment of the soul calls to the wandering Gypsy, for we find refreshment not in a single draught but in many draughts drunk in the White Hills in the company of kindred spirits.

Campfire Memories

Remember the youthful days in Romania during the Maiden Fair on Gaina Mountain in July in the Apuseni Mountains, or autumn, when we all celebrated Sait Dumitru, the holiday of the flocks of sheep returning from the mountains. Here we are celebrating the White Mountains of New Hampshire.

Many evenings around the campfire, one member of the family would share an old Gypsy folk tale, which had been passed down from past generations to the present. Many who told the stories were the elders, and their closing stories were totally reminiscent of home.

However, all that remains are the rotted tent pins and van enclosing a rusty heap of mold that once was a fragrant couch of evergreens inviting

Campsite for evening meal, postcard.

tired men to rest. The families bid farewell to the campsite and move on. Our Gypsy families have seen many campsites in the mountains, but for a moment we reflect that the woods still echo with the laughter, music and dance of the Gypsies.

Chapter 5

THE GYPSY TOURS IN NEW HAMPSHIRE

By Motorcycle

Nothing stands out more beautifully than the majestic White Mountains as they welcome visitors to the splendor of their natural celebration, which they offer to all.

The crystal cascades, a trip through the notches, a climb up the auto roads of Mount Washington, the solitude of the back roads in the wilderness and the Lakes Region of New Hampshire: all these natural attractions are magnified for our adventure, so cruise through the White Hills—the journey is the destination.

There are Gypsies of another kind in the White Mountains. They are the Gypsies on two wheels. This story of the Gypsies in the White Mountains would not be complete without mentioning the "Gypsy Tours" and its legacy.

As the Gypsies of Eastern Europe came to the White Mountains of New Hampshire, so the Gypsy Tours was formed for a group of cyclists to tour through the White Hills.

It was here in 1916 that a group of motorcyclists gathered in Laconia, New Hampshire, and created the first Gypsy Tour, which was organized by motorcycle shops and dealers from central and southern New England. This tour of motorcyclists spent several days traveling through the White Mountains and the Lakes Region.

According to Charlie St. Clair and Jennifer Anderson:

The Gypsy Tours mascot banner. *Courtesy of Laconia Motorcycle Club.*

The Federation of American Motorcycles (FAM) was the first group to sanction these tours in 1917, and then after it disbanded in 1919, the Motorcycle and Allied Trades Association (M&ATA) took over the sanction until the American Motorcycle Association (AMA) was formed in 1924.

The gypsy tour continued through the 1920s and the 1930s. In 1938, a motorcycle enthusiast named Fritzie Baer was instrumental in bringing the road races to Belknap Recreation Area (now Gunstock Mountain Resort) with the help of the New England Motorcycle Dealers Association. For more than thirty years, Baer worked hard at keeping the Laconia motorcycle rally at full steam.

In 1917, the Gypsy Tours became an overnight event, with organized trips through the White Mountains and the Lakes Region of the Granite State. The term "Gypsy" was used because the riders would travel long distances and often spend the nights in tents around a campfire by the side of the road or in a campsite. Gypsy Tours were held in different parts of the country and often took place on the same weekend each year.

History of a Nomadic Culture

The purpose of the Gypsy Tours was to provide a good time for the riders, with special events and smaller side road trips. An article in the June 1922 issue of the *Harley-Davidson Enthusiast* detailed the goals as follows:

> *First—To promote good fellowship among the riders of all makes of motorcycles and to give them a pleasure tour worth talking about until the time for the next tour rolls around.*
>
> *Second—To give the general public a convincing demonstration of the practical transportation and pleasure possibilities of the motorcycle. The more tours there are and the more riders there are in each tour, the more effective the demonstration will be.*

In June 1918, the National Motorcycle Gypsy Tour watch fob award was presented by FAM to those with a "perfect score." The perfect score award was given out to the winners of an

> *endurance run, which was a long-distance motorcycle course over public roads, typically 300 to 350 miles in length, that was run over two consecutive days, and that featured checkpoints (controls) about every 505 miles. Given the poor road conditions and general unreliability of motorcycles at the time, this was clearly not an easy task! An endurance run is a very complicated affair. The men have to pass certain points at a given time, and not before that time. On the run they are subjected to a hill-climbing test and also to a secret brake test. There is a score of 1,000 points, from which various deductions are made. The great honor, of course, is to make a perfect score (1,000 points). To achieve this reflects high credit on both the man and machine...What is the most needed in a run of this sort is a cool head and plenty of nerve. It was the reckless drivers who came to grief—the men who, instead of taking the affair calmly, rushed madly along the course, hoping to gain time for repairs between one control and another, if any were needed.*

Riders who arrived ahead of time at a control had committed as much of an offense as finishing behind time and were penalized accordingly.

Typically, the "survivors" who were able to complete the endurance run received bronze medals; riders with high, but not perfect, scores received silver medals, while the riders achieving perfect scores received gold medals. The rider with not only a perfect score but also the "most consistent riding" and/or "neatest appearance" would receive the coveted diamond award.

According to historian Joanne Cram:

On August 1, 1924 the American Motorcycle Association was officially established. The following year, the AMA took over from the M&ATA the sponsorship of the Gypsy Tours, and greatly expanded them, from perhaps a few events to over separate ones. With the exception of the World War II period, the Gypsy Tours were yearly events that continued until the early 1960s. At that time, even though many of the gatherings that they were based on continued "Gypsy Tours" fell out of favor, and was replaced by the term "Tour and Rally," as in "New England Tour & Rally."

In 1991, the term Gypsy Tours was officially revived by the AMA. However, by this time, the individual events had all gone their own way in naming themselves. In 1953, or perhaps even earlier, Laconia first called its event Motorcycle Week, and that term has stuck to the current day.

The various motorcycle organizations and vendors that came to these events have been selling souvenirs since the earliest years of the Laconia rally. Souvenirs specifically marked "Laconia" can be seen here. Many others souvenirs were marked "Gypsy Tours" but were not tagged with the Laconia name. The generic souvenirs were sold not only at the Laconia rally but at other Gypsy Tours as well.

Motorcycle Racing

According to Charlie St. Clair and Jennifer Anderson's book *Laconia Motorcycle Week*:

Motorcycle racing, hill climbs, and drag racing were happening at Laconia right from the first year of the gypsy tours. With no courses for these events to take place, they were often held wherever they could be safely done.

Tower Hill at Weirs Beach was famous for riders racing their motorcycles up the hill. Motorcycle races were held between riders anywhere the road was good. That all changed in 1938.

In 1938, motorcycle racing began at the Belknap Mountain Recreation Area in the town of Gilford, New Hampshire. Fritzie Baer was instrumental

One-hundred-mile National Championship Road Race in 1946. In St. Clair and Anderson's *Images of America: Laconia Motorcycle Week*, this caption appeared with this photo: "In this race of 1946 are pictured here Ben Campanale on No. 2, Bill Anderson on No. 8, Ted Edwards on No. 13, Ed Kretz on No. 1, Jim Chann on No. 6, Bill Miller on No. 14, and Albert Wolfe on No. 12. Note the crowd of spectators along the course." Photo by Butch Baer. *Courtesy of Charlie St. Clair and Jennifer Anderson.*

in bringing the race to the Laconia area from Old Orchard, Maine. The 1938 National Championship race was unusual in many respects. It was considered to be the first official National Championship race in Laconia. It was the only two-hundred-mile race ever to be held in Laconia. This race was held in September rather than the usual time in June.

Before the advent of motorcycle racing at the Belknap Mountain Recreation Area in Gilford in 1938, the New England Gypsy Tour officially took place in Laconia. During the first three years of racing, from 1938 to 1941, Laconia was still considered the official center of the rally. For the first time in 1941, Gilford became an official part of the rally and was advertised as "Weirs, N.H.–Gilford, N.H." After World War II, from 1946 to 1949, official programs referred to the "Laconia–Gilford" rally. From 1952 onward, the official program covers dropped Gilford and proclaimed the rally as the "Laconia" rally.

The rally became tightly associated with the racing in Gilford because of the many non-race activities that took place at the Belknap Mountain

Motorcycling Digest

Official Organ of the New England Motorcycle Dealers' Association, Inc.

VOL. XIII   WEYMOUTH 89, MASSACHUSETTS   NUMBER 3

Official Program

27th Annual
New England Gypsy Tour

●————and————●

100-Mile National Championship Road Race

LACONIA - GILFORD, N. H.
JUNE 21, 22, 1947

Motorcycling Digest (1947). *Courtesy of Charlie St. Clair and Jennifer Anderson and the Laconia Motorcycle Week Association.*

Recreation Area during the 1940s and 1950s. Now, only a small percentage of motorcyclists who visit Laconia for the rally actually attend the races, now located in Loudon, New Hampshire.

The cover of *Motorcycling Digest* and the accompanying caption were graciously provided by Charlie St. Clair and Jennifer Anderson from *Laconia Motorcycle Week*, published by Arcadia Publishing in 2008. It reads as follows:

> *This cover of the 1947* Motorcycling Digest, *which was the official program of the New England Motorcycle Dealer's Association, served as the official program for the Gypsy Tour and the 100-mile National Championship Road Race at Belknap Recreation Area. In programs such as this one, a rider saw advertisements from local businesses and others in or around New England, pictures from previous tours and races, and detailed information about what would be going on. The New England Motorcycle Dealer's Association sponsored both the Gypsy Tour and the national road races at Laconia for decades. On this cover, it says the 27th annual, but the races and the gypsy tour were not held during the war years from 1942 through 1945. Because of this, Laconia Motorcycle Week was no longer considered an annual rally. Today the New England Harley-Davidson Dealer's Association is the offshoot of the original New England Motorcycle Dealers' Association. (Courtesy of the Laconia Motorcycle Week Association.)*

A list of Gypsy Tours in 1952 from the May issue of the *American Motorcycling Magazine* includes "The Black Hills Classic in Sturgis," which eventually became the largest motorcycle rally in the country, overtaking the Laconia rally during the 1970s–1980s. It started in 1930 as a Gypsy Tour, twenty-two years after Laconia's first Gypsy Tour. The second-largest United States rally, in Daytona, which began in 1937, was always associated with racing rather than a Gypsy Tour. Presently, Laconia is the third-largest rally in the country.

In the foreword of the 1955 program, Fritzie Baer boasted:

> *There is no doubt in the minds of any motorcycle rider in the United States that Laconia today is synonymous with the greatest Gypsy Tour and motorcycle race to be held anyplace in the country. This is a beautiful set up whereby the racing fraternity from the novice rider through the amateur and into the expert class all have an opportunity of racing on this world famous mountain track.*

In 1965, the first motorcycle race at the Bryar Motor Sports Park in Loudon, New Hampshire, took place. Racing has continued at this location until the present day. In 1990, when the Bryar racetrack was replaced by the New Hampshire International Speedway, the first professional race at the newly opened facility was the Sixty-seventh Annual Loudon Classic, held on June 17 of that year. On November 2, 2007, the track was purchased by Speedway Motor Sports Inc. and renamed the New Hampshire Motor Speedway. The Loudon Classic presently occurs on the first Sunday of Motorcycle Week, during the second week in June each year.

Times had changed, and a period of turbulence affected most all Americans during the 1960s. Motorcycle clubs were no exception. The media featured motorcyclists as lower-class citizens, fitting the stereotype of the Hell's Angels. In 1963, the Belknap Recreation Area closed the area and cancelled all events for the year. Many motorcyclists became very upset by the unwelcoming greeting they received.

However, the Laconia Bike Week did see times of trouble. During the summer of 1965, a riot between motorcycle gangs and the local law enforcement broke out. This event brought national attention to Laconia. The rally was eventually reduced to a three-day weekend, and public support declined, evidenced by the reduced numbers of participants.

Speaking of a very unfortunate event that took place, historians Charlie St. Clair and Jennifer Anderson wrote, "The so-called riot at Weirs Beach happened in 1965. By the time the Associated Press picked up the story and sent it over the wires, many thought half the city of Laconia had been destroyed."

Unfortunately, in 1966, after the riot at Weirs Beach, the entire area looked like a military zone, with the National Guard and other law enforcement highly visible. In that same year, the Laconia City Council passed an ordinance prohibiting drinking in public. The ordinance stated, "No person shall drink any alcoholic beverages...on any public street or public highway, public sidewalk, municipal parking lot, or municipal park within the limits of the City of Laconia."

This ordinance killed the celebratory atmosphere that year; thus, the rally began to decline and drivers were slow to return to Weirs Beach.

Charlie St. Clair and Jennifer Anderson continued, "Motorcycle Weekend was born in 1966, since all events except the races were canceled. One day of events meant the crowds from around the country were no longer coming. Fritzie Baer and others like Keith Bryar kept the rally going with a lot of effort."

It was not until 1991 that the Laconia Motorcycle Association was formed by area businesses and organizations in an effort to increase tourism in the

Laconia area. The role of the not-for-profit association was to promote motorcycle week and bring back visitors from around the world to partake in events happening all over the state of New Hampshire. Local businesses approached the Federation of American Motorcyclists for its support in order to bring the rally back to a weeklong event. Eventually the local business owners joined with the local motorcycle groups and founded the Laconia Motorcycle Rally and Race Association, which organizes and schedules all events associated with motorcycle week. The Laconia Motorcycle Week is now a nine-day event, which officially ends on Father's Day.

POW-MIA FREEDOM RIDE

According to Charlie St. Clair and Jennifer Anderson:

The POW-MIA Freedom Ride has grown to become one of the most popular rides that take place during motorcycle week in Laconia. The ride was formed under the guidance of Robert Jones of Meredith, Jack Hayes, other members of the HD Riders Motorcycle Club and Paul Lessard. The

Postcard view of the Presidential Range in the White Mountains from the Androscogin Valley.

ride formed in what was the Lakes Region Plaza, now the Winnipesaukee Crossing in Gilford. Every year, several hundred riders take a ride from the starting point and ride up Weirs Boulevard, down Lakeside Avenue, out Scenic Road to Watson Road, and north on U.S. Route 3 to Hesky Park in Meredith. Hesky Park is the site of the POW-MIA Northeast Network vigil. The parade is escorted by local and state police officers.

According to historian Joanne Cram:

In 1998, the Laconia Rally celebrated its 75th running, placing it among one of America's longest running events. In 1995 hosted its first American Motorcycle Association Grand National Road Race. The tradition continues today as motorcyclists gather annually in the AMA Superbike Series and the famous Laconia rally, hosted by the American Motorcycle Association Chartered Lakeside Sharks Motorcycle Club.

APPENDIX

Gypsy Folk Tales

The following tales are not all Romani but are collected from Gypsy folk tales from other countries, namely Turkey, Wales, Transylvania, Poland, Bukowina, Bohemia, England and Scotland. Most of the stories were shared around the world as well as at the Gypsy campsites as their nightly entertainment in the White Mountains of New Hampshire.

Most of these stories have common themes, such as the mystic, mythology, magic, death, murder and the supernatural.

In 1899, Francis Hindes Groome carefully collected and assembled a portfolio entitled *Gypsy Folk Tales*. This collection of forgotten tales was published by Hurst and Blackett, and these cherished tales are related here.

THE PRINCE AND THE WIZARD

A Romani Gypsy Folk Story

There was a king, and he had an only son. Now, that lad was heroic, nought-heeding. And he set out in quest of heroic achievements. And he went a long time nought-heeding. And he came to a forest, and lay down to sleep in the shadow of a tree, and slept. Then he saw a dream, that he arises and goes to the hill where the dragon's horses are, and that if you keep straight on you will come to the man with no kidneys, screaming and roaring. Se he arose and departed, and came to the man with no kidneys. And when he came there, he asked him, "Mercy! What are you screaming for?"

He said, "Why. A wizard has taken my kidneys, and has left me here in the road as you see me."

Then the lad said to him, "Wait a bit longer till I return."

And he left him, and journeyed three more days and three nights. And he came to that hill, and sat down, and ate, and rested. And he arose and went to the hill. And the horses, when they saw him, ran to eat him. And the lad said, "Do not eat me, for I will give you pearly hay and fresh water."

Then the horses said, "Be our master. But see you do as you've promised."

The lad said. "Horses, if I don't, why, eat me and slay me."

So he took them and departed with the horses. And he put them in the stable, and gave them fresh water and pearly hay. And he mounted the smallest horse, and set out for the man with no kidneys, and found him there. And he asked him what was the name of the wizard who had taken his kidneys.

"What his name is I know not, but I do know where he is gone to. He is gone to the other world."

Then the lad took and went a long time nought-heeding, and came to the edge of the earth, and let himself down, and came to the other world. And he went to the wizard's there, and said, "Come forth, O wizard, that I may see the sort of man you are."

So when the wizard heard, he came forth to eat him and slay him. Then the lad took his heroic club and his sabre; and the instant he hurled his club, the wizard's hands were bound behind his back. And the lad said to him, "Here. You wizard, tell quick, my brother's kidneys, or I slay thee this very hour."

And the wizard said, "They are there in a jar, Go and get them.'

And the lad said, "And when I've got them, what am I to do with them?"

The wizard said, "Why, when you've got them, put them in water and give him them to drink."

Then the lad went and took them, and departed to him. And he put the kidneys in water, and gave him to drink, and he drank. And when he had drunk he was whole. And he took the lad, and kissed him, and said, "Be my brother till my death or thine, and so too in the world to come."

So they became brothers. And having done so, they took and journeyed in quest of heroic achievements. So they set out and slew every man that they found in their road. Then the man who had no kidneys said he was going after the wizard, and would pass to the other world. Then they took and went there to the edge of the earth, and let themselves in. And they came there, and went to the wizard. And when they got there, how they set themselves to fight, and fought with him two whole days. Then when the lad, his brother, took and hurled his club, the wizard's hands were bound behind his back. And he cut his throat, and took his horses, and made then two apples.

And they went further, and came on a certain house, and there were three maidens. And the lad hurled his club, and carried away half their house. And when the maidens saw that, they came out, and saw them coming. And they flung a comb in their path, and it became a forest—no needle could thread it. So when the lad saw that, he flung his club and his sabre. And the sabre cut and the club battered. And it cut all the forest till nothing was left.

And when the maidens saw that they had felled the forest, they flung a whetstone, and it became a forest of stone, so that there was no getting further. And he flung the club, and demolished the stone, and made dust of it. And when the maidens saw that they had demolished the stone, they flung a mirror before them, and it became a lake, and there was no getting over. And the lad flung his sabre, and it cleft the water, and they passed through, and went there to the maidens. When they came there they said, "And what were you playing your cantrips on us for, maidens?"

The maidens said, "Why, lad, we thought that you were coming to kill us."

Then the lad shook hands with them, the three sisters, and said to them, "There maidens, and will you have us?"

And they took them to wife—one for himself, and one for him who had lost his kidneys, and one they gave to another lad. And he went with them home. And they made a marriage.

And I came away, and I have told the story.

THE APPLES OF PREGNANCY

A Romani Gypsy Folk Story

Note: This is the exact and true original wording as found in the text.

There were where there were a king and a queen. Now for sixteen years the king and the queen had had no sons or daughters. So he thought they would never have any. And he was always weeping and lamenting, for what would become of them without any children? Then the king said to the queen, "O queen, I will go away and leave you, and if I do not find a son born of you by my return, know that either I will kill you with my own hands, or I will send you away, and live no longer with you."

Then another king sent a challenge to him to go and fight, for, if he goes not, he will come and slay him on his throne. Then the king said to his queen, "Here, O queen, is a challenge come for me to go and fight. If I had had a son, would he not have gone, and I have remained at home?"

She said, "How can I help it, O king, if God has not chosen to give us any sons? What can I do?"

He said, "Prate not to me of God. If I come and don't find a son born of you I shall kill you."

And the king departed.

Then the holy God and St. Peter fell to discussing what they should do for the queen. So God said to Peter, "Here, you Peter, go down with this apple, and pass before the window, and cry, 'I have an apple, and whoso eats of it will conceive.' She will hear you. For it were a pity, Peter, for the king to come and kill her."

So St. Peter took the apple, and came down, and did as God had told him. He cried in front of the queen's window. She heard him, and came out, and called him to her, and asked, "How much do you want for the apple, my man?"

He said, "I want much, give me a purse of money."

And the queen took the purse of money, and gave it him, and took the apple and ate it. And when she had eaten it, she conceived. And St. Peter left her the purse of money there. So the time drew near for her to bear a child. And the very day that she brought forth her son, his father came from the war, and he had won the fight. So when he came home and heard that the queen had borne him a son, he went to the wine-shop and drank till he was drunk. And as he was coming home from the wine-shop, he reached the door, and fell down and died. Then the boy heard it, and rose up out of his mother's arms, and went to the vintner, and killed him with a blow. And he came home. And the people, the nobles, beheld him, what a hero he was, and wondered at him. But an evil eye fell on him, and for three days he took to his bed. And he died of the evil eye.

THE CREATION OF THE VIOLIN

A Transylvanian Gypsy Folk Story

In a hut on a mountain, in a fair forest, lived a girl with her four brothers, her father, and her mother. The sister loved a handsome rich huntsman, who often ranged the forest, but who would never speak to the pretty girl. Mara wept day and night, because the handsome man never came near her. She often spoke to him, but he never answered, and went on his way. She sang the song:

> *Dear man from a far country*
> *Slip your hand into mine*
> *Clasp me, if you will, in your arms*
> *Lovingly will I kiss you.*

She sang it often and often, but he paid no heed.

Knowing now no other succor, she called the devil. "O devil, help me."

The devil came, holding a mirror in his hand, and asked what she wanted. Mara told him her story and bemoaned to him her sorrow.

"If that's all," said the devil, "I can help you. I'll give you this. Show it to your beloved and you'll entice him to you."

Once again came the huntsman to the forest, and Mara had the mirror in her hand and went to meet him. When the huntsman saw himself in the mirror, he cried, "Oh! That's the devil, that is the devil's doing; I see myself." And he ran away, and came no more to the forest.

Mara wept now and again day and night, for the handsome man never came near her. Knowing now no other succour for her grief, she called again the devil. "O devil, help me." The devil came and asked what she wanted. Mara told how the huntsman had run away, when he saw himself in the mirror. The devil laughed and said, "Let him run, I shall catch him; like you, he belongs to me. For you both have looked in the mirror, and whoso looks in the mirror is mine. And now I will help you, but you must give me your four brothers, or help you I cannot." The devil went away and came back at night, when the four brothers slept, and made four strings of them, fiddle strings—one thicker, then one thinner, the third thinner still, and the thinnest the fourth. Then said the devil, "Give me also your father."

Mara said, "Good, I will give you my father, only you must help me."

Of the father the devil made a box, that was the fiddle. Then he said, "Give me also your mother."

Mara answered, "Good, I give you also my mother, only you must help me."

The devil smiled, and made of the mother a stick, and horsehair of her hair: this was the fiddle-stick (bow). Then the devil played, and Mara rejoiced. But the devil played on and on, and Mara wept.

Now laughed the devil and said, "When your beloved comes, play, and you will entice him to you."

Mara played, and the huntsman heard her playing and came to her. In nine days came the devil and said, "Worship me, I am your lord."

They would not, and the devil carried them off. The fiddle remained in the forest lying on the ground, and a poor Gypsy came by and saw it. He played, and as he played in thorp and town they laughed and wept just as he chose.

God's Godson

A Romani Gypsy Folk Story

There was a queen. From youth to old age that queen never bore but one son. That son was a hero. So soon as he was born, he said to his father, "Father, have you no sword or club?"

"No my child, but I will order one to be made for you."

The son said, "Don't order one, father: I will go just as I am."

So the son took and departed, and journeyed a long while, and took no heed, till he came into the great forest. So in that forest he stretched himself beneath a tree to rest a bit, for he was weary. And he sat there a while. Then the holy God and St. Peter came on the lad; and he was un-baptized. So the holy God asked him, "Where are you going, my lad?"

"I am going in quest of heroic achievements, old fellow."

Then the holy god thought and thought, and made a church. And he caused sleep to fall on the lad, and bade St. Peter lift him, and went with him to the church, and gave him the name Handak. And the holy God said to him, "Godson, a hero like you there shall never be any other; and do you take my god-daughter."

For there was a maiden, equally heroic, and baptized by God. And she was his god-daughter, and he told his godson to take her. And he gave him a wand of good fortune and a sword. And he endowed him with strength, and set him down. And his godfather departed to heaven, like the holy God that he was.

And Handak perceived that God had endowed him with strength, and he set out in quest of heroic achievements, and journeyed a long while, and took no heed. So he came into a great forest. And there was a dragon three hundred years old. And his eyelashes reached down to the ground, and likewise his hair. And the lad went to him and said, "All hail."

"You are welcome."

Soon as that hero [the dragon] heard his voice, he knew that it was God's godson.

And the lad, Handak, asked him, "Does God's god-daughter dwell far hence?"

"She dwells not far; it is but a three days' journey."

And the lad took and departed, and journeyed three days until he came to the maiden's aid. Soon as the maiden saw him, she recognized him for her godfather's godson. And she let him into her house, and served up food to him, and ate with him and asked him, "What seek you here, Handak?"

He said, "I have come on purpose to marry you."

"With whom?"

"With myself and you will."

She said, "I will not have it so without a fight."

And the lad said, "Come let us fight."

And they fell to fighting, and fought three days; and the lad vanquished her. And he took her, and went to their godfather. And he crowned them and made a marriage. And they became rulers over all lands. And I came away, and told the story.

The Vampire

A Romani Gypsy Folk Story

There was an old woman in a village. And grown-up maidens met and span, and made a "bee." And the young sparks came and laid hold of the girls, and pulled them out and kissed them. But one girl had no sweetheart to lay hold of her and kiss her. And she was a strapping lass, the daughter of wealthy peasants; but three whole days no one came near her. And she looked at the big girls, her comrades. And no one troubled himself with her. Yet she was a pretty girl, a prettier was not to be found. Then came a young spark, and took in his arms and kissed her, and stayed with her until cock-crow. And when the crock crowed at dawn he departed. The old woman saw he had cock's feet. And she kept looking at the lad's feet, and she said, "Nita, my lass, did you see anything?"

"I didn't notice."

"Then didn't I see he had cock's feet?"

"Let be mother, I didn't see it."

And the girl went home and slept; and she arose and went off to the spinning, where many more girls were holding a "bee." And the young sparks came, and took each of his sweethearts. And they kissed them, and stayed awhile, and went home. And the girl's handsome young spark came and took her in his arms and kissed her and pulled her about, and stayed with her till midnight. And the cock began to crow. The young spark heard the cock crowing, and departed. What said the old woman who was in the hut, "Nita, did you notice that he had horse's hoofs?"

"And if he had, I didn't see."

Then the girl departed to her home. And she slept and arose in the morning, and did her work that she had to do. And night came, and she took her spindle and went to the old woman in the hut. And the other girls came, and the young sparks came, and each laid hold of his sweetheart. But the pretty girl looks at them. Then the young spark gave over and departed home. And the only girl remained neither a long time nor a short time. Then came the young girl's spark. Then what will the girl do? She took heed and stuck a needle and thread in his back. And he departed when the cock crew, and she knew not where he had gone. Then the girl arose in the morning and took the thread, and followed up the thread, and saw him in a grave where he was sitting. Then the girl trembled and went back home. At night the young spark that was in the grave came to the old woman's house and saw that the girl was not there. He asked the old woman, "Where's Nita?"

"She has not come."

Then he went to Nita's house, where she lived, and called, "Nita, are you at home?"

Nita answered, "I am."

"Tell me what you saw when you came to the church. For if you don't tell me I will kill your father."

"I didn't see anything."

Then he looked, and he killed her father, and departed to his grave.

Next night he came back. "Nita, tell me what you saw."

"I didn't see anything."

"Tell me or I will kill your mother, as I killed your father. Tell me what you saw."

"I didn't see anything."

Then he killed her mother, and departed to his grave. Then the girl arose in the morning. And she had twelve servants. And she said to them, "See, I have much money and many oxen and many sheep; and they shall come to the twelve of you as a gift, for I shall die tonight. And it will fare ill with you if you bury me not in the forest at the foot of an apple tree."

At night came the young spark from the grave and asked, "Nita, are you at home?"

"I am."

"Tell me, Nita, what you saw three days ago, or I will kill you, as I killed your parents."

"I have nothing to tell you."

Then he took and killed her. Then, casting a look, he departed to his grave.

So the servants, when they arose in the morning, found Nita dead. The servants took her and laid her out decently. They sat and made a hole in the wall and passed her through the hole, and carried her, as she had bidden, and buried her in the forest by the apple tree.

And half a year passed by, and a prince went to go and course hares with greyhounds and other dogs. And he went to hunt, and the hounds ranged the forest and came to the maiden's grave. And a flower grew out of it, the like of which for beauty there was not in the whole kingdom. So the hounds came on her monument, where she was buried, and they began to bark and scratched at the maiden's grave. Then the prince took and called the dogs with his horn, and the dogs came not. The prince said, "Go quickly thither."

Four huntsmen arose and came and saw the flower burning like a candle. They returned to the prince, and he asked them, "What is it?"

"It is a flower, the like was never seen."

The lad heard, and came to the maiden's grave, and saw the flower and plucked it. And he came home and showed it to his father and mother. Then he took and put it in a vase at his bed-head where he slept. Then the flower arose from the vase and turned a somersault, and became a full-grown maiden. And she took the lad and kissed him, and bit him and pulled him about, and slept with him in her arms, and put her hand under his head. And he knew it not. When the dawn came she became a flower again.

In the morning the lad rose up sick, and complained to his father and mother, "Mammy, my shoulders hurt me, and my head hurts me."

His mother went and brought a wise woman and tended him. He asked for something to eat and drink. And he waited a bit, and then went to his business that he had to do. And he went home again at night. And he ate and drank and laid himself down on his couch, and sleep seized him. Then the flower arose and again became a full-grown maiden. And she took him again in her arms, and slept with him, and sat with him in her arms. And he slept. And she went back to the vase. And he arose, and his bones hurt him, and he told his mother and father. Then his father said to his wife, "It began with the coming of the flower. Something must be the matter, for the boy is quite ill. Let us watch tonight, and post ourselves on one side, and see who comes to our son."

Night came, and the prince laid himself in his bed to sleep. Then the maiden arose from the vase, and became there was never anything more fair—as burns the flame of a candle. And his mother and his father, the king saw the maiden, and laid hands on her. Then the prince arose out of his sleep, and saw the maiden that she was fair. Then he took her in his arms and kissed her, and lay down in his bed, slept till day.

And they made a marriage and ate and drank. The folk marveled, for a being so fair as that maiden was not to be found in the realm. And he dwelt with her half a year, and she bore a golden boy, two apples in his hand. And it pleased the prince well.

Then her old sweetheart heard it, the vampire who had made love to her, and had killed her. He arose and came to her and asked her, "Nita, tell me, what did you see me doing?"

"I didn't see anything."

"Tell me truly, or I will kill your child, your little boy, as I killed your father and mother. Tell me truly."

"I have nothing to say to you."

And he killed her boy. And she arose and carried him to the church and buried him.

At night the vampire came again and asked her, "Tell me, Nita, what you saw."

"I didn't see anything."

"Tell me, or I will kill the lord whom you have wedded."

Then Nita arose and said, "It shall not happen that you kill my lord. God send you burst."

The vampire heard what Nita said, and burst. Ay, he died, and burst. In the morning Nita arose and saw the floor swimming two hand's-breadth deep in blood. Then Nita bade father-in-law take out the vampire's heart with all speed. Her father-in-law, the king, hearkened, and opened him and took out his heart, and gave it into Nita's hand. And she went to the grave of her boy and dug the boy up, applied the heart, and the boy arose. And Nita went to her father and to her mother, and anointed them with the blood, and they arose. Then, looking on them, Nita told all the troubles she had borne, and what she had suffered at the hands of the vampire.

THE BLACK LADY

A Welch Gypsy Folk Story

A young girl goes to service at an old castle with the Black Lady, who warns her not to look through the window. The black lady goes out. The girl gets bored and looks through the window, and sees the Black Lady playing cards with the devil. She falls down frightened. The Black Lady comes in and asks her what she had seen.

"Nothing saw I; naught can I say. Leave me alone; I am weary of my life."

The Black Lady beats her, and asks her again. "What saw you through the window?"

"Nothing saw I," etc. The girl runs off and meets a keeper, who takes her home, and after some years marries her. She has a child, and is bedded.

Enter the Black Lady. "What saw you through the window?"

"Nothing saw I," etc. The Black Lady takes the child, dashes its brains out, and exit.

Enter the husband. The wife offers no explanation, and the husband wants to burn her, but his mothers intercedes and saves her this time. But the same thing happens again, and the husband makes a fire. As she is being brought to the stake, the Black Lady comes.

"What saw you through the window?"

"Nothing saw I," etc.

"Take her and burn her," say the Black Lady.

They fastened her up, and bring a light. The same question, the same answer. The Black Lady see that she is secret, so gives her back her two children, and leaves her in peace.

THE THREE WISHES

A Welch Gypsy Folk Story

A fool lives with his mother. Once on a hillside he finds a young lady exposed to the heat of the sun, and twines a bower of bushes round her for protection. She awakes, and gives him three wishes. He wishes he were at home; no sooner said than done. On the way he catches a glimpse of a lovely lady at a window, and wishes idly that she were with child by him. She proves so, but knows not the cause. She bears a child, and her parents summon every one from far and near to visit her. When the fool enters, the baby says, "Dad, dad!"

Disgusted at the lover's low estate the parents cast all three adrift in a boat. The lady asks him how she became with child, and he tells her. "Then you must have a wish still left."

He wishes they were safe on shore in a fine castle of their own. They live happily there for some time, then return home, and visit the girl's parents splendidly dressed. The parents refuse to believe him the same man. He returns in his clothes. Triumph and reconciliation, he provides for his old mother.

FAIRY BRIDE

A Welch Gypsy Folk Story

A king has three sons, and knows not to which of them to leave his kingdom. They shoot for it with bow and arrows. The youngest shoots so far that his arrow is lost. He seeks it for a long time, and at last finds it sticking in a glass door. He enters and finds himself in the home of the Queen of the Fairies, whom he marries. After a while he returns home with his bride. An old witch who lived in the park incites the king to ask the fairy bride to fetch him a handkerchief, which will cover the whole park. She does it, and then is asked to bring her brother. She refuses, but finally summons him. He enters, and terrifies the king by his threatening aspect. "Why did you call me for?" The king is too frightened to answer coherently. The fairy's brother kills him and the old witch, and vanishes. They live at the castle.

THE DRAGON

A Welch Gypsy Folk Story

There was a great city, and in that city was great mourning; every day it was hung with black cloth and with red. There was in a cave a great dragon; it had four-and-twenty heads. Every day must he eat a woman—ah! God! What can be done in such a case? It is clear impossible every day to find food for that dragon. There was but one girl left. Her father was a very wealthy man; he was a king; over all kings he was lord. And there came a certain wanderer, came into the city, and asked what's new there.

They said to him, "Here is very great mourning."

"Why so? Any one dead?"

"Every day we must feed the dragon with twenty-four heads. If we failed to feed him, he would crush all the city underneath his feet."

"I'll help you out of that. It is just twelve o'clock; I will go there alone with my dog."

He had such a big dog, whatever a man just thought of, that dog immediately knew. It would have striven with the devil. When the wanderer came to the cave, he kept crying, "Dragon, come out here with your blind mother. Bread and men you have eaten, but will eat no more. I'll see if you are any good."

The dragon called him into the cave, and the wanderer said to him, "Now give me whatever I ask for to eat and to drink, and swear to me always to give that city peace, and never to eat men, no, not one. For if ever I hear of your doing so I shall come back and cut your throat."

"My good man, fear not; I swear to you, for I see you're a proper man. If you weren't I should long since have eaten up you and your dog. They tell me what you want of me."

"I only want you to bring me the finest wine to drink, and meat such as no man has ever eaten. If you don't, you will see I shall destroy everything that is yours, shall shut you up here, and you will never come out of this cave."

"Good, I will fetch a basket of meat, and forthwith cook it for you."

He went and brought him such meat as not man ever had eaten. When he had eaten and drunk his fill, then the dragon must swear to him never to eat anybody, but sooner to die of hunger.

"Good, so let us leave it."

He went back, that man, who thus had delivered the city, so that it had peace. Then all the gentlemen asked him what he wanted for doing so well. The dragon from that hour never ate any one. And if they are not dead they are still alive.

Note: It was the custom for English Gypsy women to wear black and red during mourning.

STORY OF THE BRIDGE

A Turkish Gypsy Folk Story

In olden days there were twelve brothers. And the eldest brother, the carpenter Manoli, was making the long bridge. One side he makes; one side falls. The twelve brothers had one mistress, and they all had to do with her. They called her to them, "Dear bride." On her head was the ray; in her hands was a child. Whoseso wife came first, she will come to the twelve brothers. Manoli's wife, Lenga, will come to the twelve brothers. Said his wife, "Thou hast not eaten bread with me. What has befallen thee that thou eatest not bread with me? My ring has fallen into the water. Go fetch my ring." Her husband said, "I will fetch thy ring out of the water." Up to his two breasts came the water in the depth of the bridge there. He came into the fountain and he was drowned. Beneath he became a talisman, the innermost arch of the bridge. "God send a wind to blow, that the tray may fall from the head of her who bears it in front of Lenga."

A snake crept out before Lenga, and she feared, and said, "Now have I fear at sight of the snake, and am sick. Now it is not bad for my children?" She bowed herself over the sea, where the carpenter Manoli made the bridge. Another man called Manoli's wife; with him she went on the road. There, when they went on the road, he went to the tavern, he was weary; the man went, drank the juice of the grape, got drunk. Before getting home, he killed Manoli's wife, Lenga.

The Two Children

A Bukowina Gypsy Folk Story

Somewhere there was a hunter's son, a soldier, and there was also a shoemaker's daughter. She had a dream that if he took her to wife, and if she fell pregnant by him, she would bring forth twins—the boy with a golden star upon his breast, and the girl with a golden star upon the brow. And he presently took her to wife. And she was poor, that shoemaker's daughter; and he was rich. So his parents did not like her for a daughter-in-law. She became with child to him; and he went off to serve as a soldier. Within a year she brought forth. When that befell, she had twins exactly as she had said. She bore a boy and a girl; the boy had a golden star upon his breast, and the girl had a golden star upon her brow. But his parents threw the twins into diamond chests, wrote a label for each of them, and put it in the chest. Then they let them swim away down the Vah River.

Then my God so ordered it, that there were two fishers, catching fish. They saw those chests come swimming down the river; they laid hold of both of them. When they had done so, they opened the chest, and there were the children alive, and on each was the label with writing. The fishers took them up, and went straight to the church to baptize them.

So those children lived to their eighth year, and went already to school. And the fishers had also children of their own, and used to beat them, those foundlings. He, the boy, was called Jankos; and she, Marishka.

And Marishka said to Jankos, "Let us go, Jankos mine, somewhere into the world."

Then they went into the forest, there spent the night. There they made a fire, and Marishka fell into a slumber, whilst he, Jankos, kept up the fire. There came a very old stranger to him, and he says to him, says that stranger, "Come with me, Jankos, I will give you plenty of money."

He brought him into a vault; there a stone door opened before him; the vault was full, brim full of money, Jankos took two armfuls of money. It was my God who was there with him, and showed him the money. He took as much as he could carry, then returned to Marishka. Marishka was up already and awake; she was weeping—"Where, then, is Jankos?"

Jankos calls to her, "Fear not, I am here; I am bringing you plenty of money."

My God had told him to take as much money as he wants; the door will always be open to him. Then they, Jankos and Marishka, went to the city; he bought clothes for himself and for her, and bought himself a fine house. Then he bought also horses and a small carriage. Then he went to the vault for that money, and helped himself again. With the shovel he flung it on the carriage; then he returned home with so much money that he didn't know what to do with it.

Then he ordered a band to play music, and arranged for a ball. Then he invited all the gentry in that country, invited all of them; and his parents too came. This he did that he might find out who were his parents. Right enough they came; and he, Jankos, at once knew his mother—my God had ordained it, that he at once should know her. Then he asks his mother, does Jankos, what a man deserves who ruins two souls, and is himself alive.

And she says, the old lady, "Such a one deserves nothing better than to have light set to the fagot-pile, and himself pitched into the fire."

That was just what they did to them, pitched them into the fire, and he remained there with Marishka. And the gentleman cried then, "Hurrah! Bravo! That's capital."

BOBBY RAG

An English Gypsy Folk Story

Yeahs an' yeahs an' double yeahs ago, deah wuz a nice Gypsy gal playin' round an ole oak tree. An' up comed a squire as she wuz a-playin', an' he failed in love wid, an' asked her of she'd go to his hall an' marry him. An' she says, "No, sir, you wouldn't have a pooah Gypsy gal like me." But he meaned so, an' stoled her away an' married her.

Now when he bring'd her home, his mother warn't greeable to let hisself down so low as to marry a Gypsy gal. So she says, "You'll have to go an' stry her in de Hunderd Mile Wood, an' strip her star'-mother-naked, an' bring back her clothes an' her heart and pluck wid you."

An'he took'd his hoss, an' she jumped up behint him, and rid behint him into de wood. You'll be shuah it wor a wood, an ole-fashioned wood we know it should be, wid bears an' eagles an' sneks an' wolfs into it. An' when he took'd her in de wood he says, "Now, I'll ha' to kill you here, an' strip you star'-mother-naked and tek back your clothes an' your heart an' pluck wid me, and show dem to my mammy."

But she begged hard for herself, an' she says, "Deah's an eagle dat wood, an' he's gat de same heart an' pluck as a Christ'n; take dat home an' show it to your mammy, an' Ill gin you my clothes as well."

So he stripet her clothes affer her, an' he kilt de eagle, an' took'd his heart an' pluck home, an' showed it to his mammy, an' said as he'd kilt her.

An' she heared him rode aff, an' she wents an' she wents an, she wents an' she crep an' crep an her poor hens and knees, tell she fun' a way troo de long wood. You 'ah shuah she'd have hard work to fin' a way troo it; an' long an' by last she got to de hedge anear de road, so as she'd hear any one go by.

Now, in de marnin' deah wuz a young genleman comed by an hoss-back an' he couldn't get his hoss by for love nor money; and she hed herself in under de hedge, for she wuz afrightened 'twor de same man come back to kill her agin, an' besides you 'ah shuah she wor ashamed of bein' naked.

An' he calls out, "Ef you 'ah a ghost, go away; but of you 'ah a livin' Christ'n, speak to me."

An' she med answer direc'ly, "I'm as good a Christ'n as you are, but not in parable [apparel]."

An' when he sin her, he pull't his dear beautiful topcoat affer him, an' put it an her. An' he says, "Jump behint me." An' she jumped behint him, an' he rid wi' her to his own gret hall. An' deah wuz no speakin' tell dey get home. He knowed she wuz deah to kilt, an' he galloped as hard as he could an his blood-hoss, tell he got to his own hall. An' when he bring'd her in, dey wur all struck stunt to see a woman naked, wid her beautiful black hair hangin' down her back in long ringlets. Deh asked her what she wuz deah fur, an' she tell'd dem, an' she tell'd dem. An' you 'ah shuah dey soon put clothes an her; an' when she wuz dressed up, deah warn't a lady in de land more han'some nor her. An'his folks wor in delight av her.

"Now," dey says, "we'll have a supper for goers an' comers an' all gentry to come at."

You'ah shuah it should be a 'spensible supper an' no savation of the money. An' deah wuz to be tales tell'd an' songs sing'ed. An' every wan dat didn't sin't a song had to tell't a tale. An' every door wuz bolted for fear any wan would mek a skip out. An' it kem to pass to dis' Gypsy gal to sing a song; an' de gentleman dat fun' her says, "Now, my pretty Gypsy gal, tell a tale."

An' de gentleman dat wuz her husband knowned her, an' didn't want her to tell a tale. An' he says, "Sing a song, my pretty Gypsy gal."

An' she says, "I won't sing a song, but I'll tell a tale." An' she says—

> *Bobby rag! Bobby rag!*
> *Rou' de oak tree—*

"Pooh! Pooh!" says her husband, "dat tale won't do." (Now de ole mother an' de son, dey knowned what wuz comin' out.)

"Go on, my pretty Gypsy gal," says de oder young gentleman. "A werry nice tale indeed."

So she goes on—

> *Bobby rag! Bobby rag!*
> *Roun'd dde oak tree.*
> *A Gypsy I wuz born'd,*
> *A lady I wuz bred;*
> *Dey made me a coffin*
> *Afore I wuz dead.*

"An' dat's de rogue deah."

An' she tell't all de tale into de party, how he wur agoin' to kill her an' tek her heart an' pluck home. An' all de genetry took't an' gibbeted him alive, both him an' his mother. An' dis young squire married her, an' med her a lady for life. Ah! Of we could know her name, an' what bred she wur, what a beautiful ting dat would be. But de tale doan' say.

Note: This Gypsy story does offer some originality to English folklore as the marriage of a poor girl by a rich man; mother's jealousy is so noted. She immediately orders Bobby Rag to take the bride into a forest, kill her and bring her heart back.

THE MAGIC SHIRT

A Scottish Tinker Gypsy Folk Story

"There was a king and a knight, as there was and will be, and as grows the fir tree, some of it crooked and some of it straight; and he was a king of Eirinn," and the old tinker, and then came a wicked stepmother, who was incited to evil by a wicked hen-wife. The son of the first queen was at school with twelve comrades, and they used to play at shinny every day with silver shinnies and a golden ball. The hen-wife, for certain curious rewards, gave the step-dame a magic shirt, and she sent it to her stepson, "Sheen Billy," and persuaded him to put it on. He refused at first, but complied at last, and the shirt was a great snake about his neck. Then he was enchanted and under spells, and all manner of adventures happened; but at last he came to the house of a wise woman who had a beautiful daughter, who fell in love with the enchanted prince, and said she must and would have him.

"It will cost much sorrow," said the mother.

"I care not," said the girl, "I must have him."

"It will cost thee thy hair."

"I care not."

"It will cost thee thy right breast."

"I care not if it should cost me my life," said the girl.

And the old woman agreed to help her to her will. A caldron was prepared and filled with plants; and the king's son was put into it and stripped to the magic shirt, and the girl was stripped to the waist. And the mother stood by with a great knife, which she gave to her daughter. Then the king's son was put down in the caldron, and the great serpent, which appeared to be a shirt about his neck, changed into its own form, and sprang on the girl and fastened on her; and she cut away the hold, and the king's son was freed from the spells. Then they were married, and a golden breast was made for the lady.

Note: It may be noted that the serpent would seem to appear to be an emblem of evil and wisdom in Celtic popular mythology.

THE DOG AND THE MAIDEN

A Transylvanian Gypsy Folk Story

There was once a poor Gypsy with a very beautiful daughter, whom he guarded like an apple of his eye, for he wanted to marry her to a chieftain. So he always kept her in the tent, where the lads and lasses sat of an evening by the fire and told stories, or beguiled the time with play and dance. Only a dog was the constant companion of this poor maiden. No one knew whom the dog belonged to, or where he came from. He had joined the band once, and thenceforth continued the trusty companion of the poor beautiful maiden.

It befell once that her father must go to a far city, to sell there his besoms, baskets, spoons, and troughs. He left his daughter with the other women in the tents on the heath and set out with the men for the city. This troubled the poor girl greatly, for no one would speak to her, as all the women envied her for her beauty and avoided her; in a word, they hated the sight of her. Only the dog remained true to her; and once, as she sat sorrowfully in front of the tent, he said, "Come let us go to the heath; there I will tell you who I really am." The girl was terrified, for she had never heard of a dog being able to speak like a man; but when the dog repeated his request, she got up and went with him out on the heath. There the dog said, "Kiss me, and I shall become a man." The girl kissed him, and lo! Before her stood a man of wondrous beauty.

He sat down beside her in the grass, and told how a fairy had turned him into a dog for trying to steal her golden apples, and how he could resume his human shape for but one night in the year, and only then if a girl kiss him first. Much more had the two to tell, and they toyed in the long grass all the livelong night. When day dawned, the girl slipped back with the dog in her tent; and the two henceforth were the very best of friends.

The poor Gypsy came back from the city to the heath, merry because he had made a good bit of money. When again he must go to the city to sell his besoms and spoons, the girl remained behind with the dog in the camp, and one night she brought forth a little white puppy. In her terror and anguish she ran to the great river, and jumped into the water. When the people sought to draw her out of the water, they could not find her corpse; and the old Gypsy, her father, would have thrown himself in too, when a handsome strange gentleman came up, and said, "I'll soon get you the body."

He took a bit of bread, kissed it, and threw it into the water. The dead girl straightway emerged from the water. The people drew the corpse to land, and bore it back to the tents, in three days' time bury it. But the strange gentleman said, "I will bring my sweetheart to life."

He took the little white puppy, the dead girl's son, and laid it on the bosom of the corpse. The puppy began to suck, and when it had sucked its full, the dead girl awoke, and, on seeing the handsome man, started up and flew into his arms, for he was her lover who had lived with her as a white dog.

All greatly rejoiced when they heard this marvelous story, and nobody thought of the little white puppy, the son of the beautiful Gipsy girl. All of a sudden they heard a baby cry; and when they looked round, they saw a little child lying in the grass. Then was the great joy indeed. The little puppy had vanished and taken human shape. So they celebrated marriage and baptism together, and lived in wealth and prosperity till their happy end.

Note: This method of searching for a drowned girl's body was done by throwing family bread on the water. This custom has been practiced for many years by non-Gypsies in England. It has been written that many orthodox Gypsies have adopted and brought this method with them from the continent.

DEATH THE SWEETHEART

A Transylvanian Gypsy Folk Story

There was once a pretty young girl with no husband, no father, no mother, no brothers, no kinfolk; they were all dead and gone. She lived alone in a hut at the end of the village; and no one came near her, and she never went near anyone.

One evening a goodly wanderer came to her, opened the door, and cried, "I am a wanderer, and have been far in the world. Here will I rest; I can no further go."

The maiden said, "Stay here, I will give thee a mattress to sleep on, and, if thou wilt, victuals and drink too."

The goodly wanderer soon lay down and said, "Now once again I sleep; it is long since I slept last."

"How long?" asked the girl; and he answered, "Dear maid, I sleep but one week in a thousand years."

The girl laughed and said, "Thou jestest, surely? Thou art a roguish fellow." But the wanderer was sound asleep.

Early the next morning he arose and said, "Thou art a pretty young girl. If thou wilt I will tarry her a whole week longer."

She gladly agreed, for already she loved the goodly wanderer. So once they were sleeping, and she roused him and said, "Dear man, I dreamt such an evil dream. I dreamt thou hadst grown cold and white, and we drove in a beautiful carriage, drawn by six white birds. Thou didst blow on a mighty horn; then dead folk came up and went with us...thou wert their king."

Then answered the goodly wanderer, "That was an evil dream."

Straightway he rose and said, "Beloved, I must go, for not a soul has died this long while in all the world. I must off, let me go."

But the girl wept and said, "Go not away; bide with me."

"I must go," he answered, "God keep thee." But as he reached her his hand, she said sobbing, "Tell me, dear man, who thou art then."

"Who knows that dies," said the wanderer, "I will askest vainly; I tell thee not who I am."

Then the girl wept and said, "I will suffer everything, only do tell me who thou art."

"Good," said the man, "then thou comest with me. I am Death." The girl shuddered and died.

Note: Of the Romani folk tales, this appears to be one of the most beautiful stories of the Gypsy Folk Tales *collection.*

GLOSSARY

E xcerpts of the following glossary of Romani words and terms were provided from Marlene Sway's *Familiar Strangers: Gypsy Life in America.*

atchin' tan: a meeting place; campground

ava: yes

bender: a temporary tent made from trees

bibi: the sister's and brother's wives, parents and grandparents (aunt, great aunt), like the concept of in-laws

bilyah: handbills; advertising; fortune-telling parlors

bori: bride or newly married woman

bujo: a swindle

chai: girl

chal: youth

chavvo: boy

costorari: a subdivision of a Gypsy tinsmith; handyman and craftsman

diklo: scarf to cover the head of a married woman

doa: mother

drab: poison

drabarimos: fortunetelling

duk: hand; palm

dukkering: fortunetelling from the hand or palm reading

gadze: male leader of his family group

gaji: non-Gypsies

ghilabari: Gypsy musicians

glata: children

grai: horse

jelling: to travel

kakka: no

kavvi: kettle

khelapen: dance

kris: Gypsy court

kumpania: a group of Gypsies living, working and traveling within the same geographical area

lavengro: writer

lilai: summer

luludi: flower

mamus: mother

meripen: death; lifespan

meski: tea

mokkadi: unclean; taboo

mullo: ghost or spirit

ofisa: a fortune telling parlor

parika tut: thank you

petulengro: smith; horseshoe maker

puv: Earth, field

Rom: refers to Gypsy people

Romani: Gypsy

romania: traditional Gypsy law

Romany: Gypsy language

Rom baro: big man or chief of a Gypsy family or group of families

romni: married Gypsy woman

shav: a young Gypsy boy

shey: a young Gypsy girl

tsera: tent

ven: winter

vesh: woods or forest

vitsa: extended families who follow the authority of a chief

waffedipen: evil

yag: fire

BIBLIOGRAPHY

Andrescu, Florin, Anda Raicu and Mihai Ogrinji. *Romania, Bucuresti.* Romania: Ad Libri, 2004.

Bean, Grace H. *The Town at the End of the Road: A History of Waterville Valley.* Canaan, NH: publisher unknown, 1960.

Belcher, Francis. *Logging Railroads of the White Mountains.* Boston: Appalachian Mountain Club, 1980.

Buckland, Raymond. *Buckland's Book of Gypsy Magic.* Newburyport, MA: Weiser Books, 2010.

Groome, Francis Hindes. *Gypsy Folk Tales.* London: Hurst & Blackett, Forgotten Books, 1899.

Liegeois, Jean-Pierre. *Gypsies, An Illustrated History.* London: SAQI, 1983.

McGinnis, R.J. *The Good Old Days.* New York: Harper & Brothers, 1960.

Robinson, William F. *Abandoned New England.* New York: Graphic Society, 1978.

Spargo, John. *Iron Mining and Smelting.* Bennington, VT: publisher unknown, 1938.

St. Clair, Charles, and Jennifer Anderson. *Images of America: Laconia Motorcycle Week.* Charleston, SC: Arcadia Publishing, 2008.

Sutherland, Anne. *Gypsies: The Hidden Americans.* New York: Free Press, 1975.

Sway, Marlene. *Familiar Strangers: Gypsy Life in America.* Chicago: University of Illinois Press, 1988.

White Mountain National Forest's Waterville Unit Plan, 1978.

INDEX

V

vagabonds 22, 32
vagrant 22
vardos 42

W

wanderlust 32
Waterville 60, 61, 63
wedding 27, 28
Weirs 84, 85, 88, 90
Weiser Books 39
Welch 91, 101, 102, 103
welfare 21, 22, 25, 28, 29, 32, 45
White Mountain Attractions 43
White Mountain National Forest
      41, 43, 119
William, Frederick I 15
witchcraft 22, 32
wizard 91, 92
Woodstock 61, 74
work 7, 18, 21, 24, 29, 34, 41, 43,
      47, 49, 53, 55, 56, 63, 71, 74,
      98
World War II 17, 84

ABOUT THE AUTHOR

D r. Bruce D. Heald, PhD, is a graduate of Boston University, the University of Massachusetts at Lowell and Columbia Pacific University. He is an adjunct associate professor at Babes-Bolyai University, Cluj, Romania, and presently an adjunct professor of American history at Plymouth State University, Plymouth, New Hampshire. Dr. Heald is presently a fellow in the International Biographical Association and the World Literary Academy in Cambridge, England. Dr. Heald is the recipient of the Gold Medal of Honor for the literary achievement from the American Biographical Institute (1993). From 2005 to 2008, he was a state representative to the General Court of New Hampshire. He resides in Meredith, New Hampshire, with his family.

Visit us at
www.historypress.net